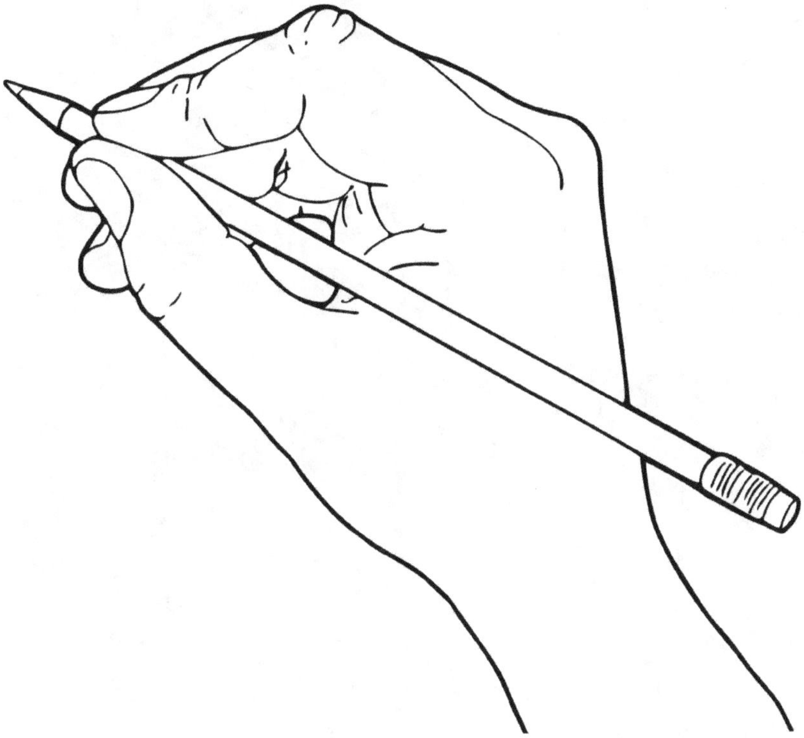

This Notebook belongs to:

________________________

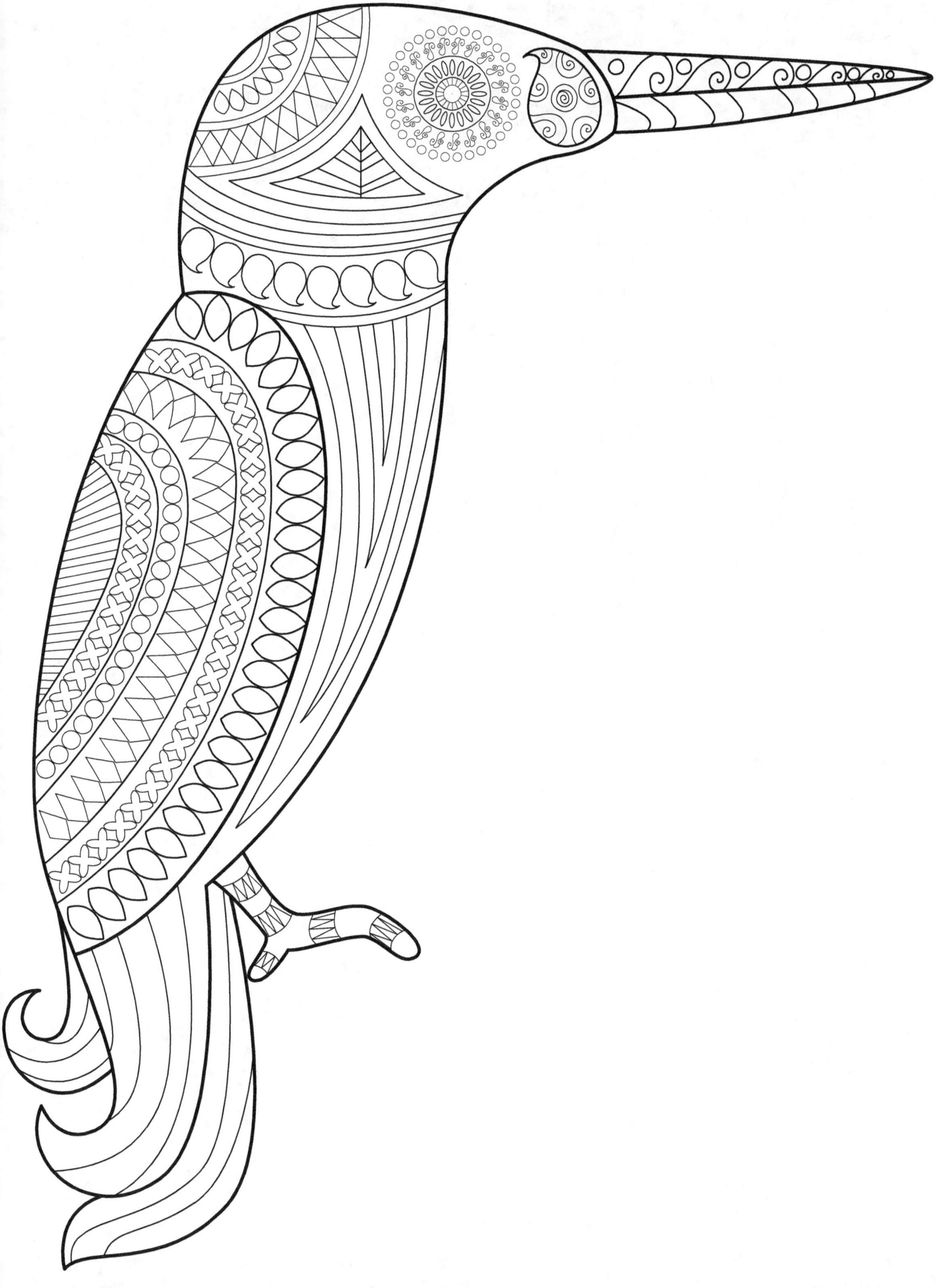

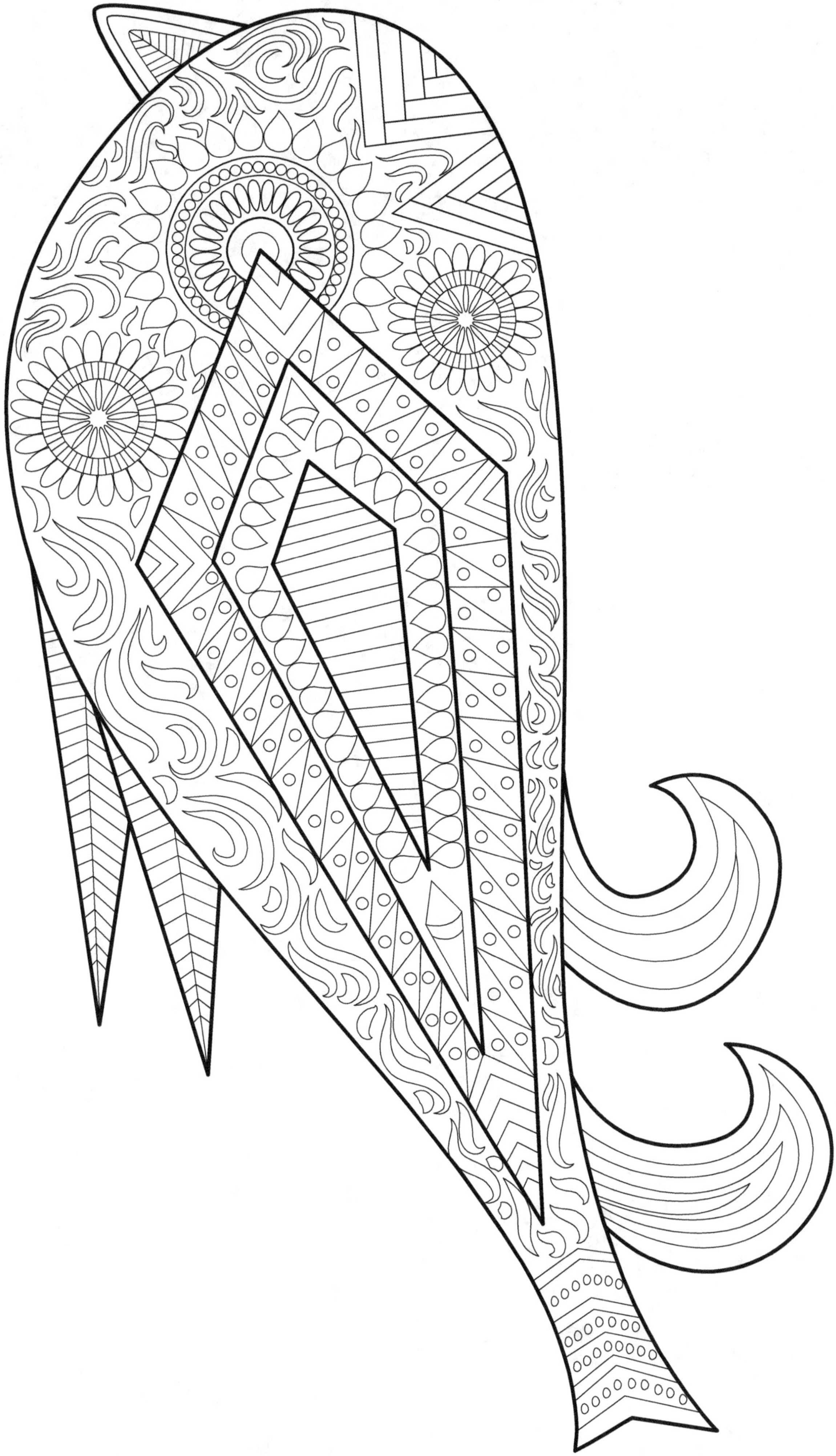

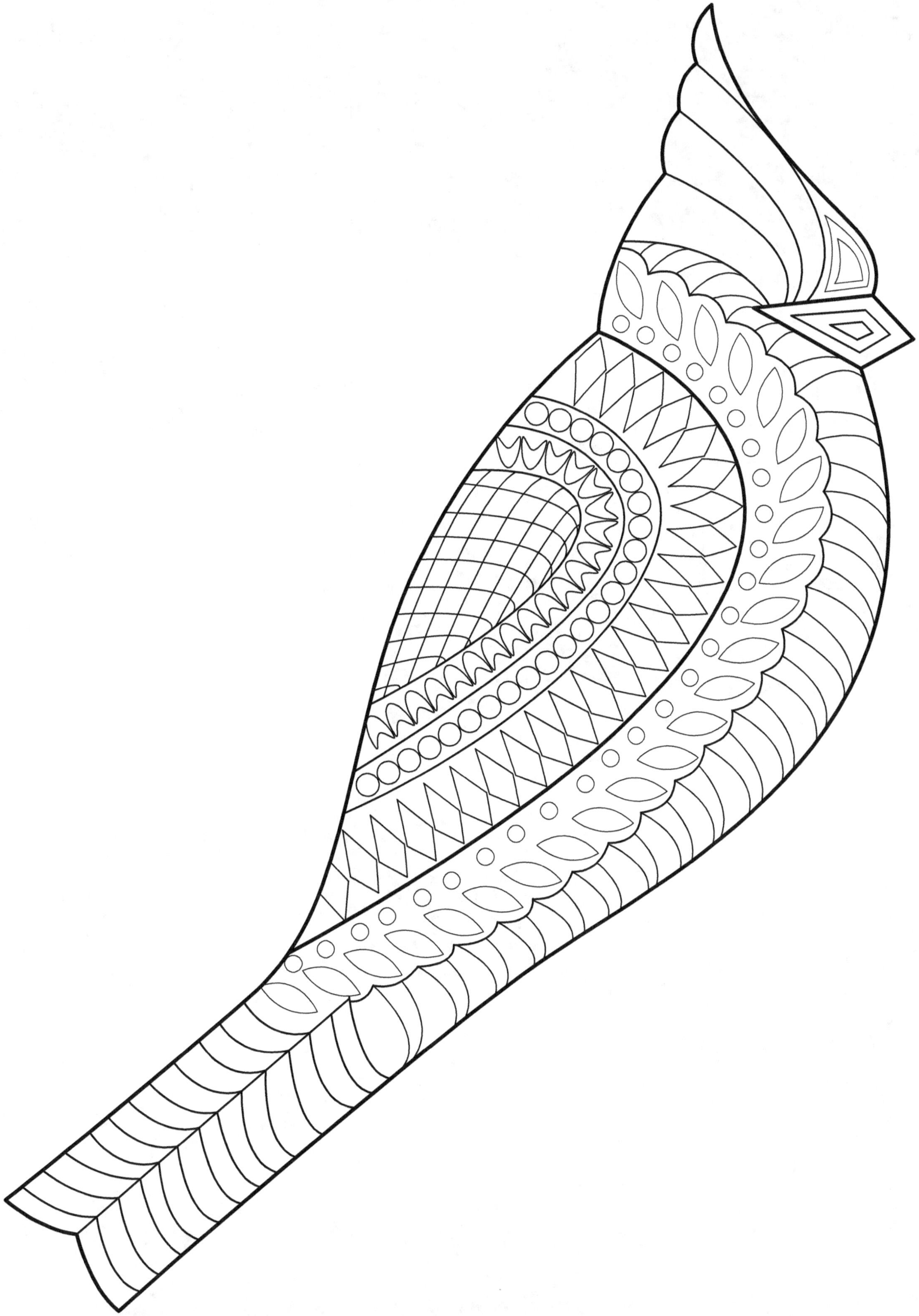

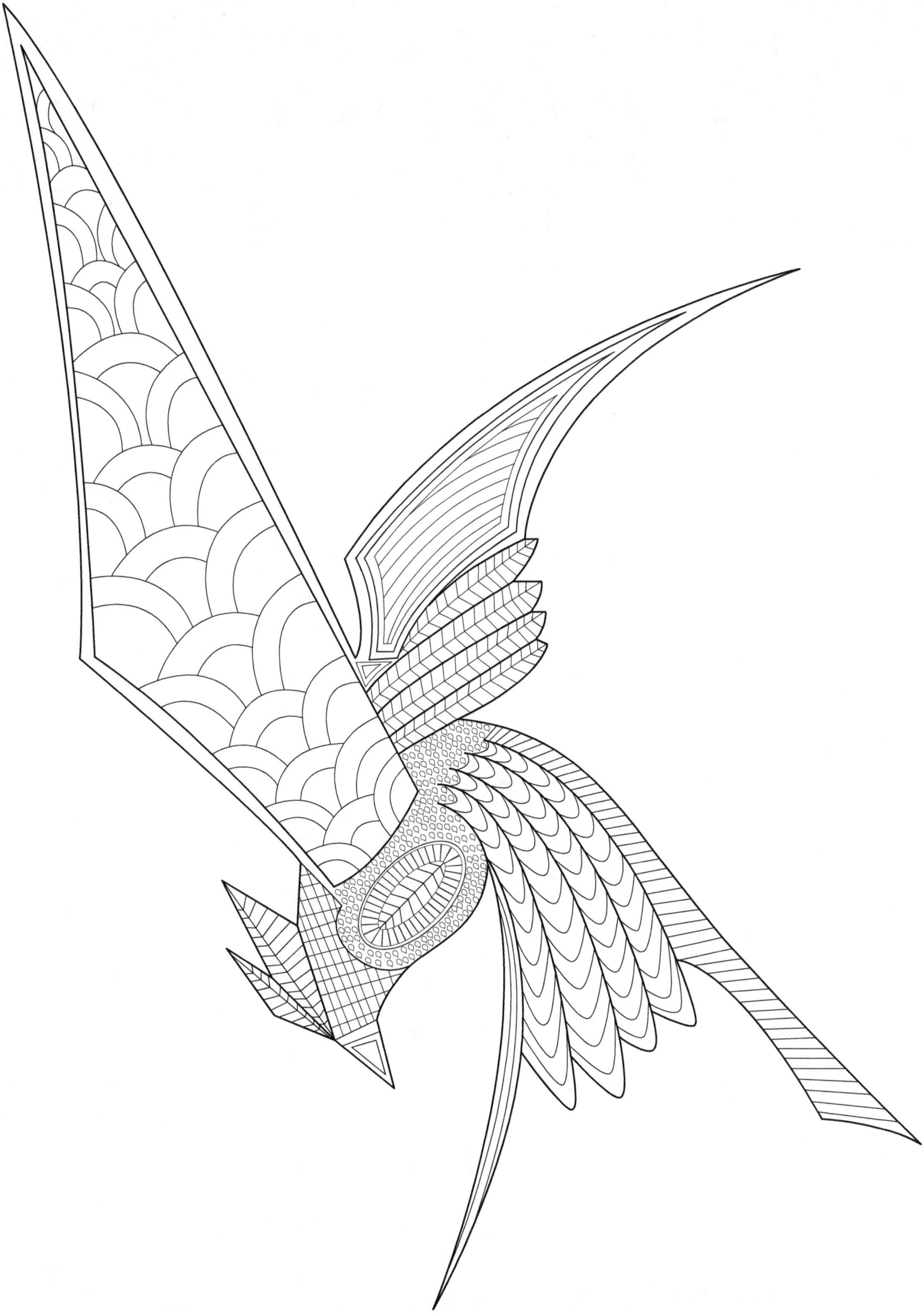

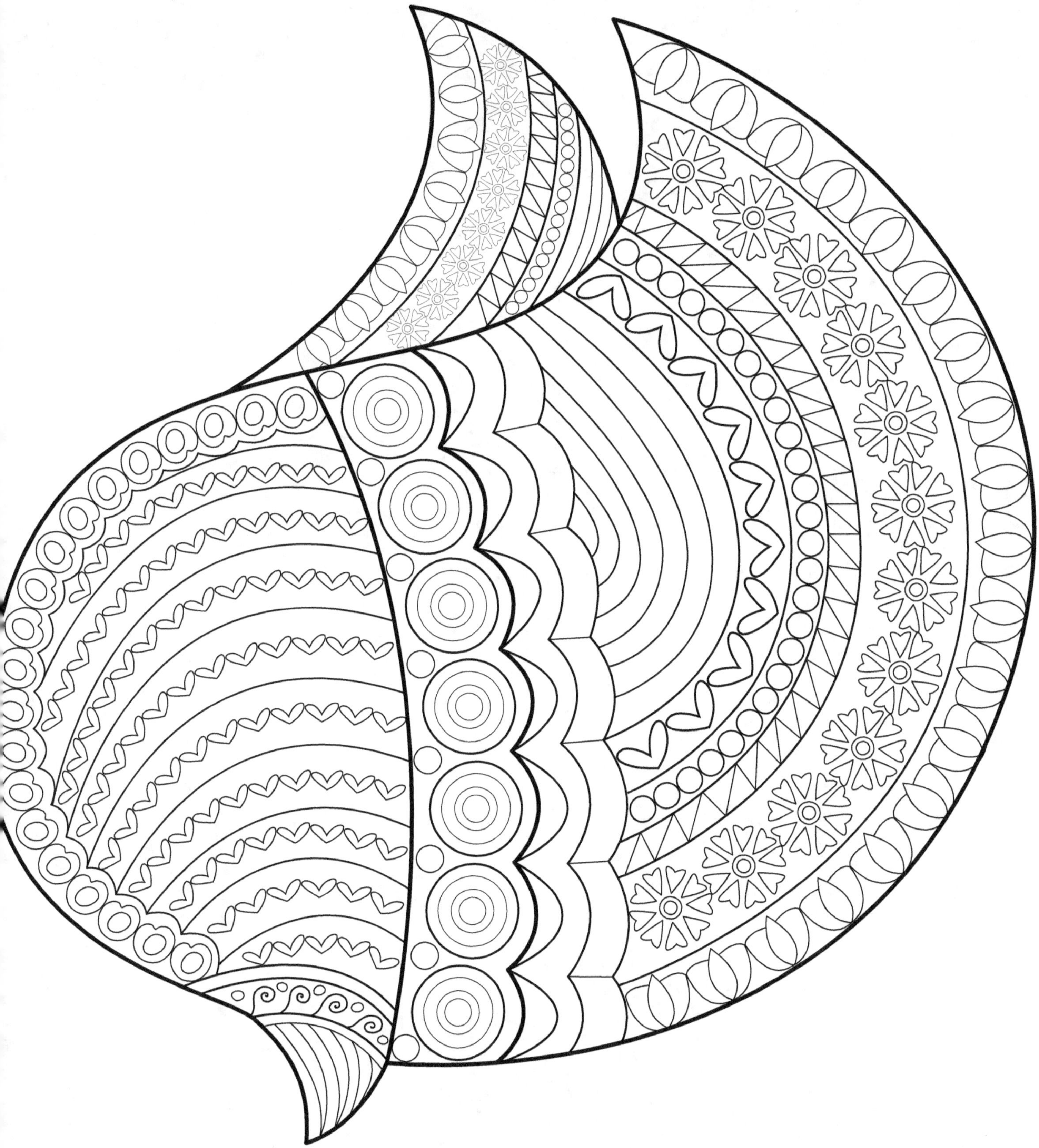

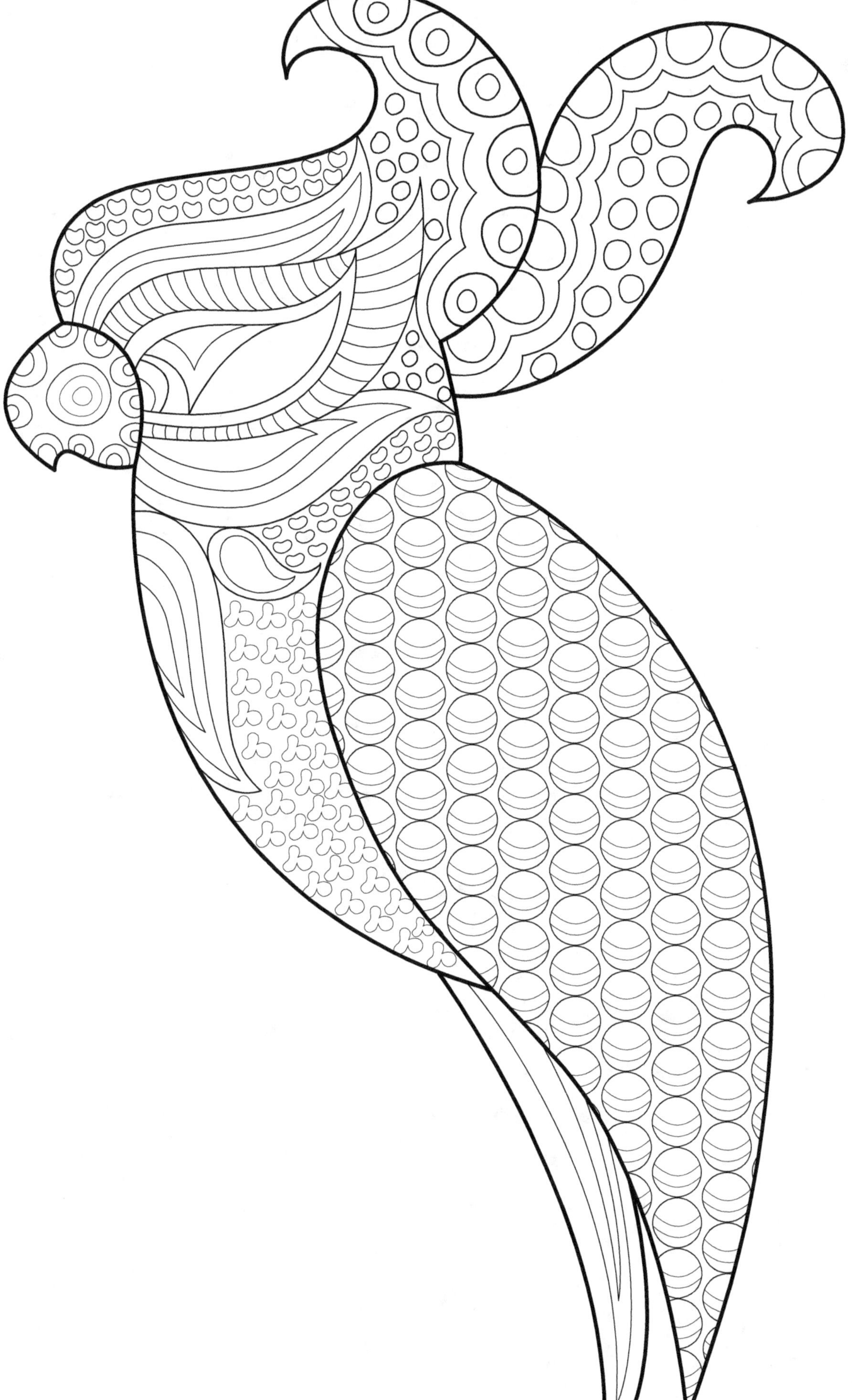

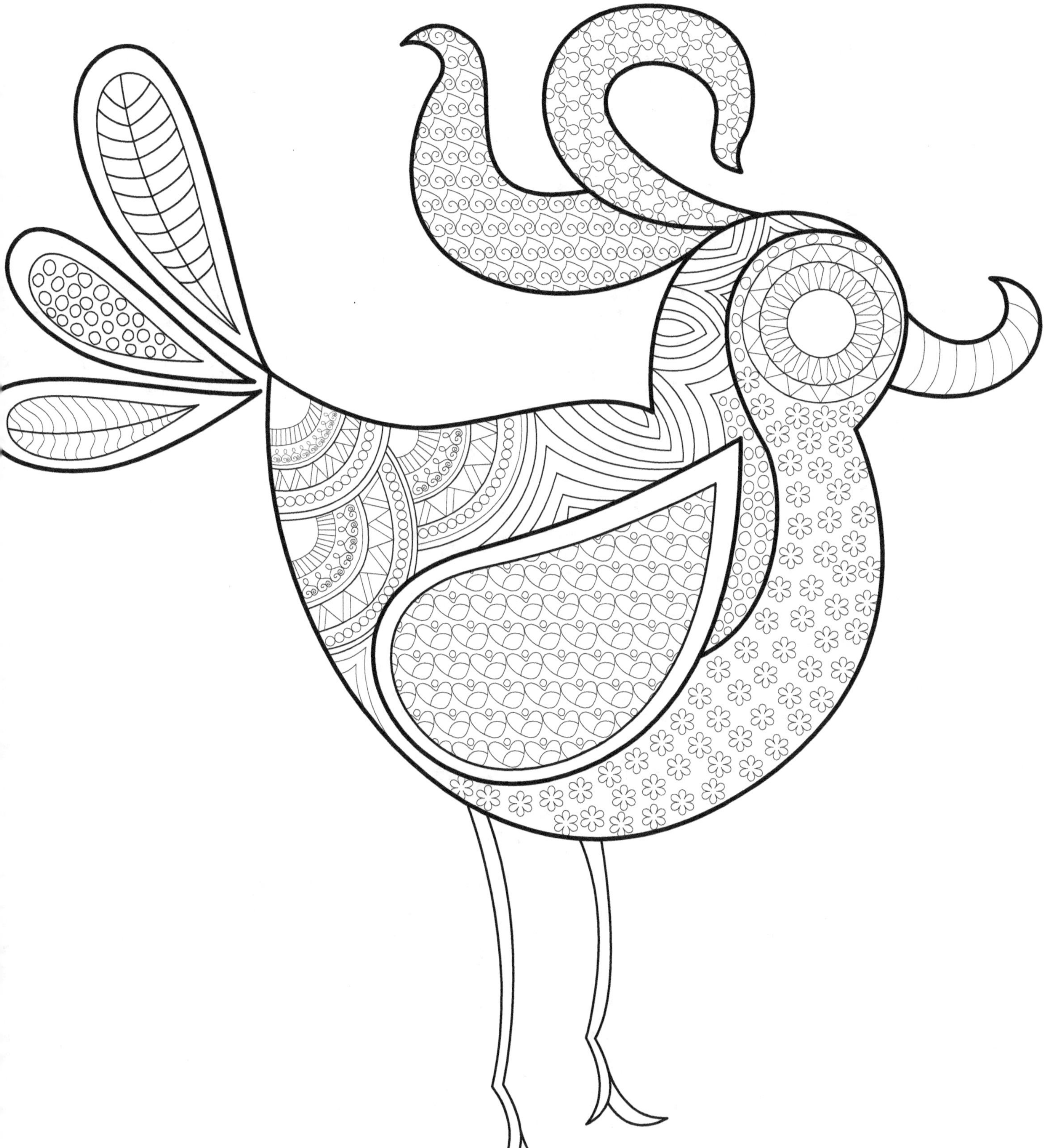

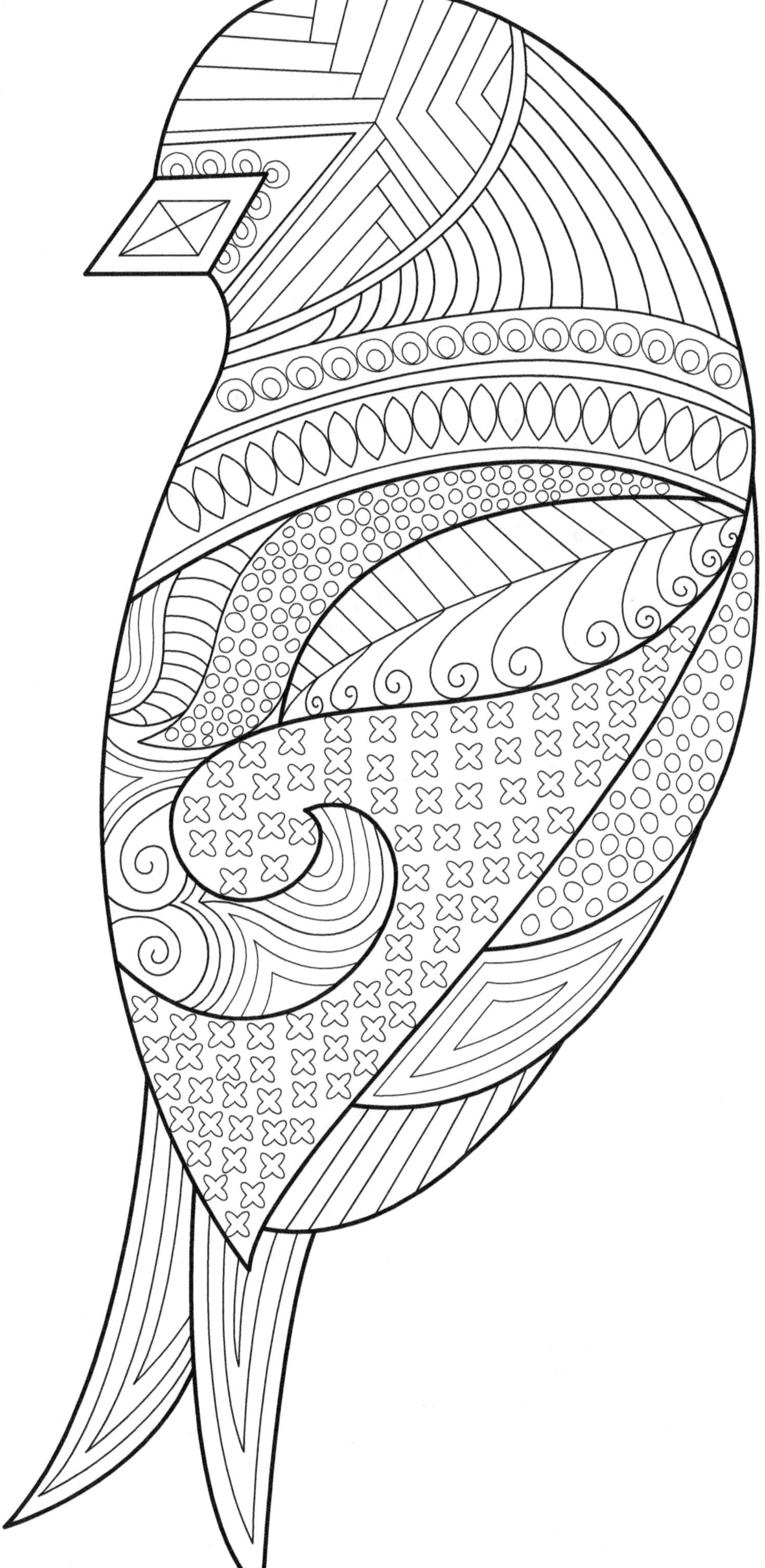

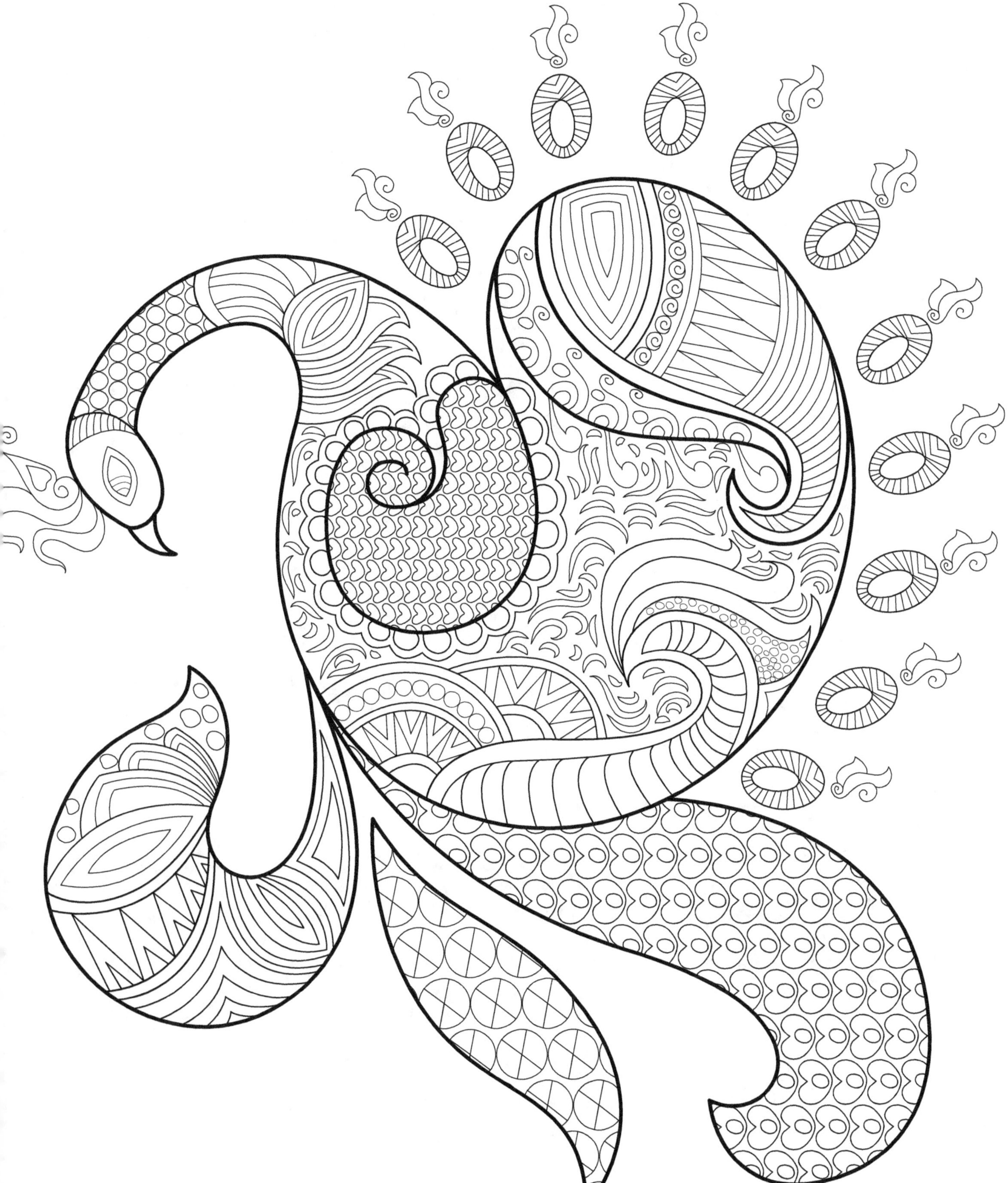

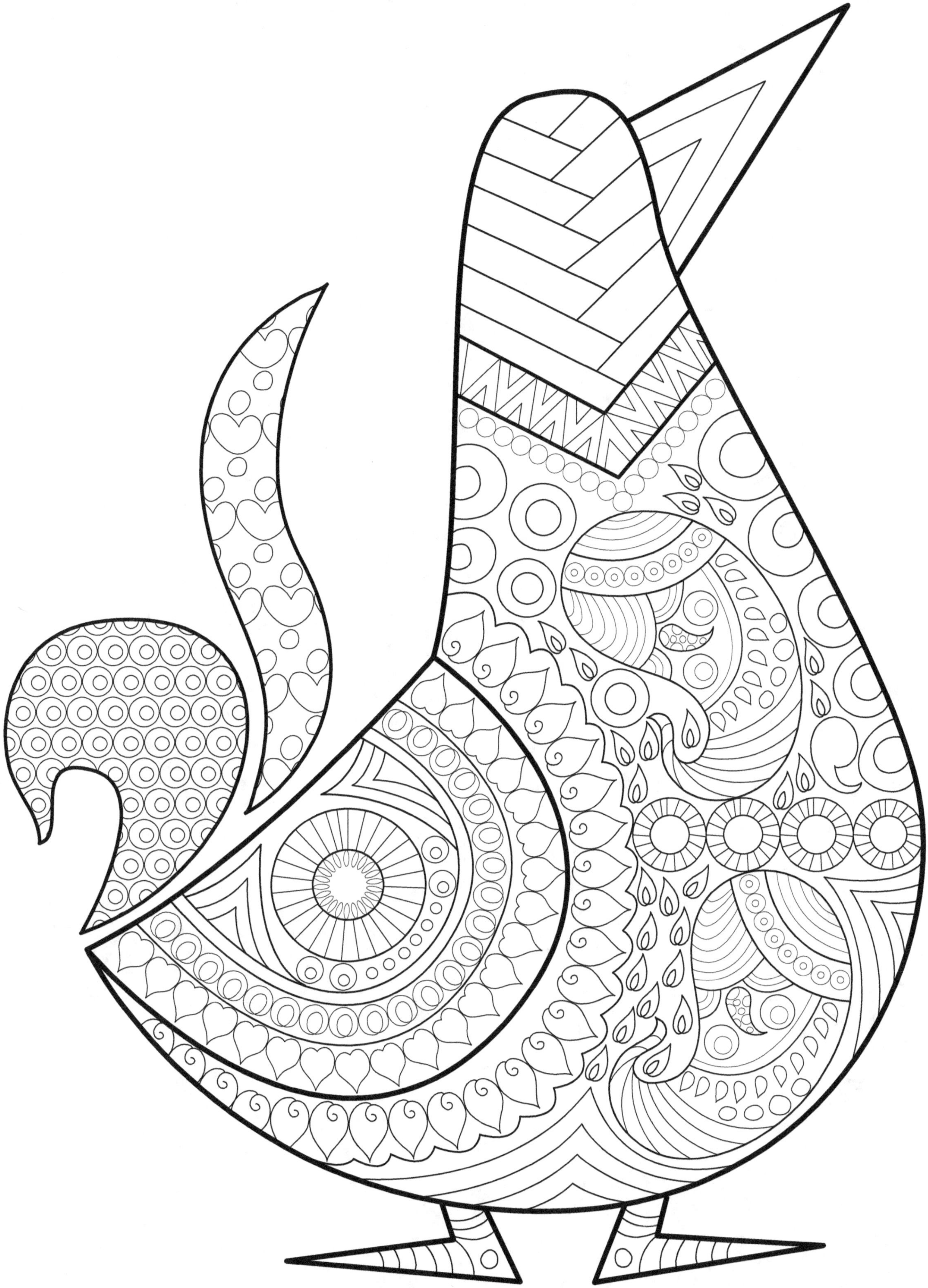

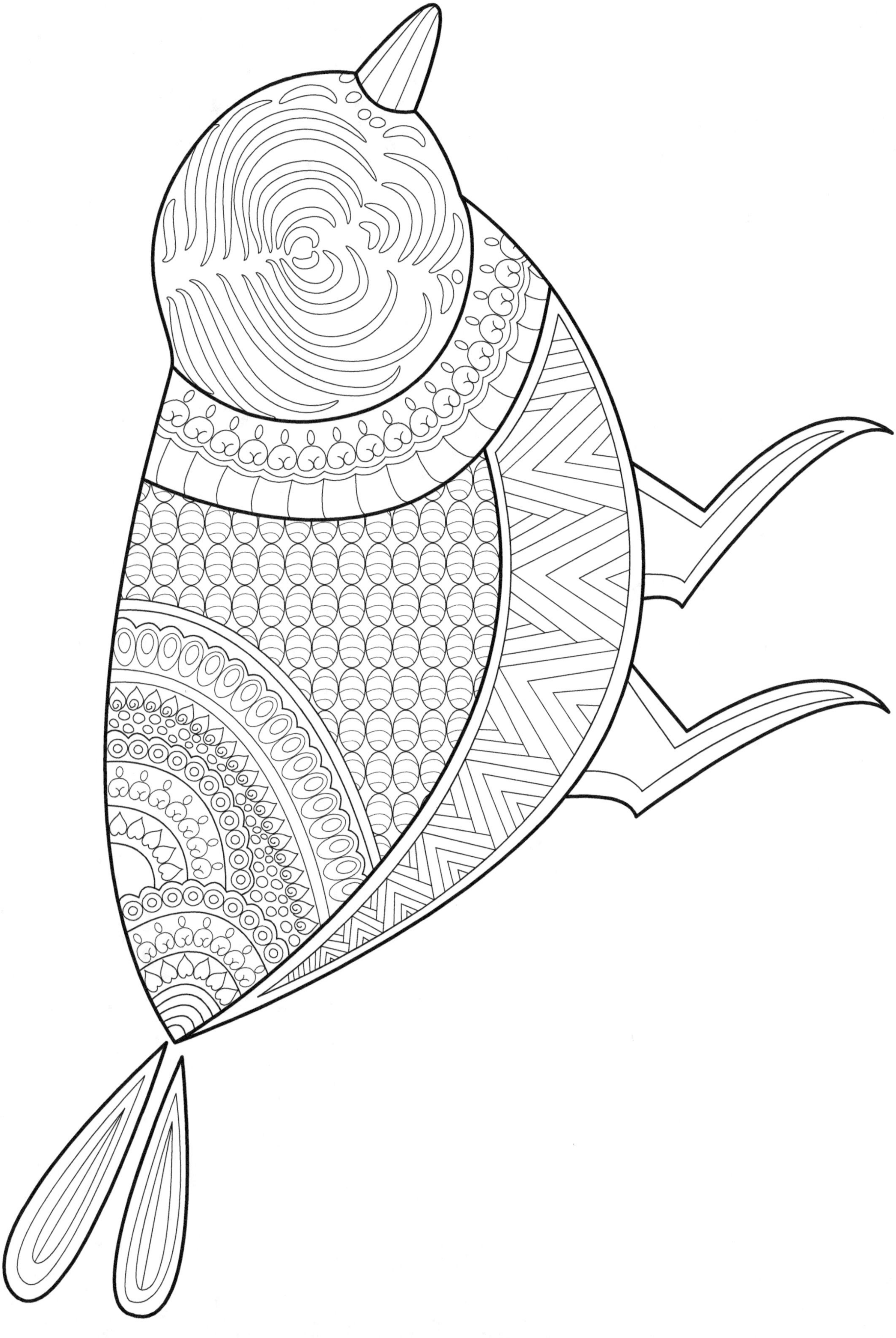

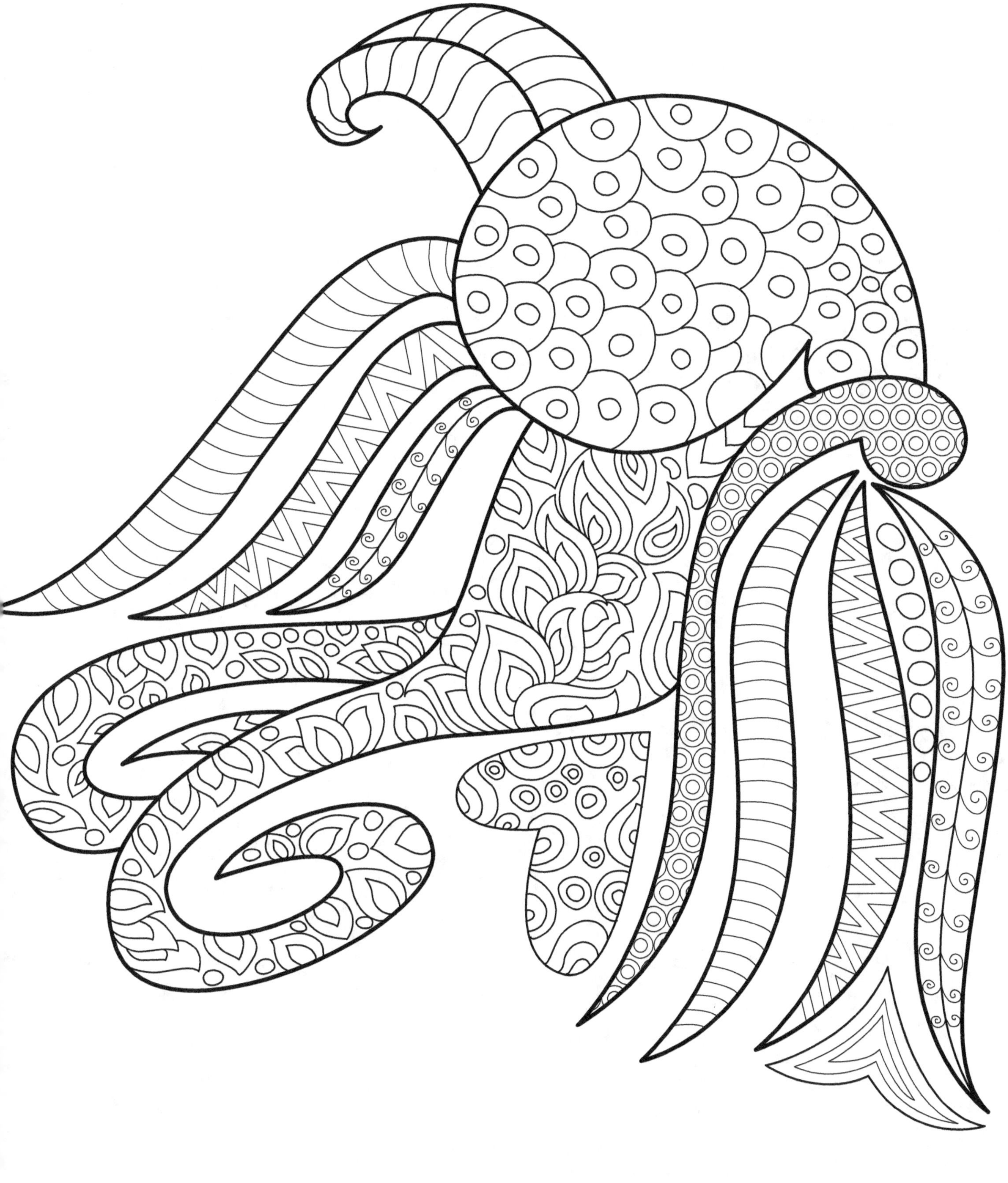

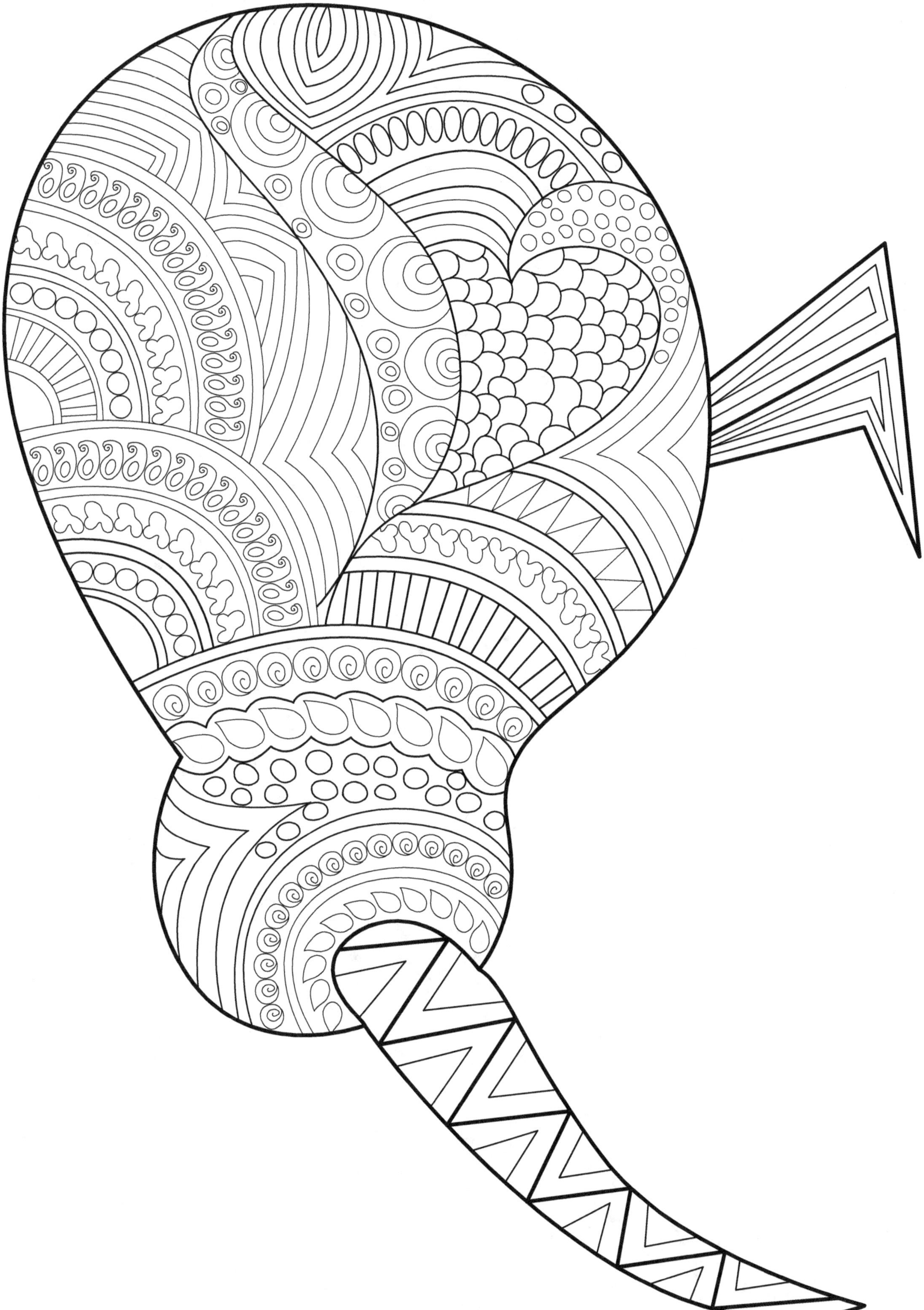

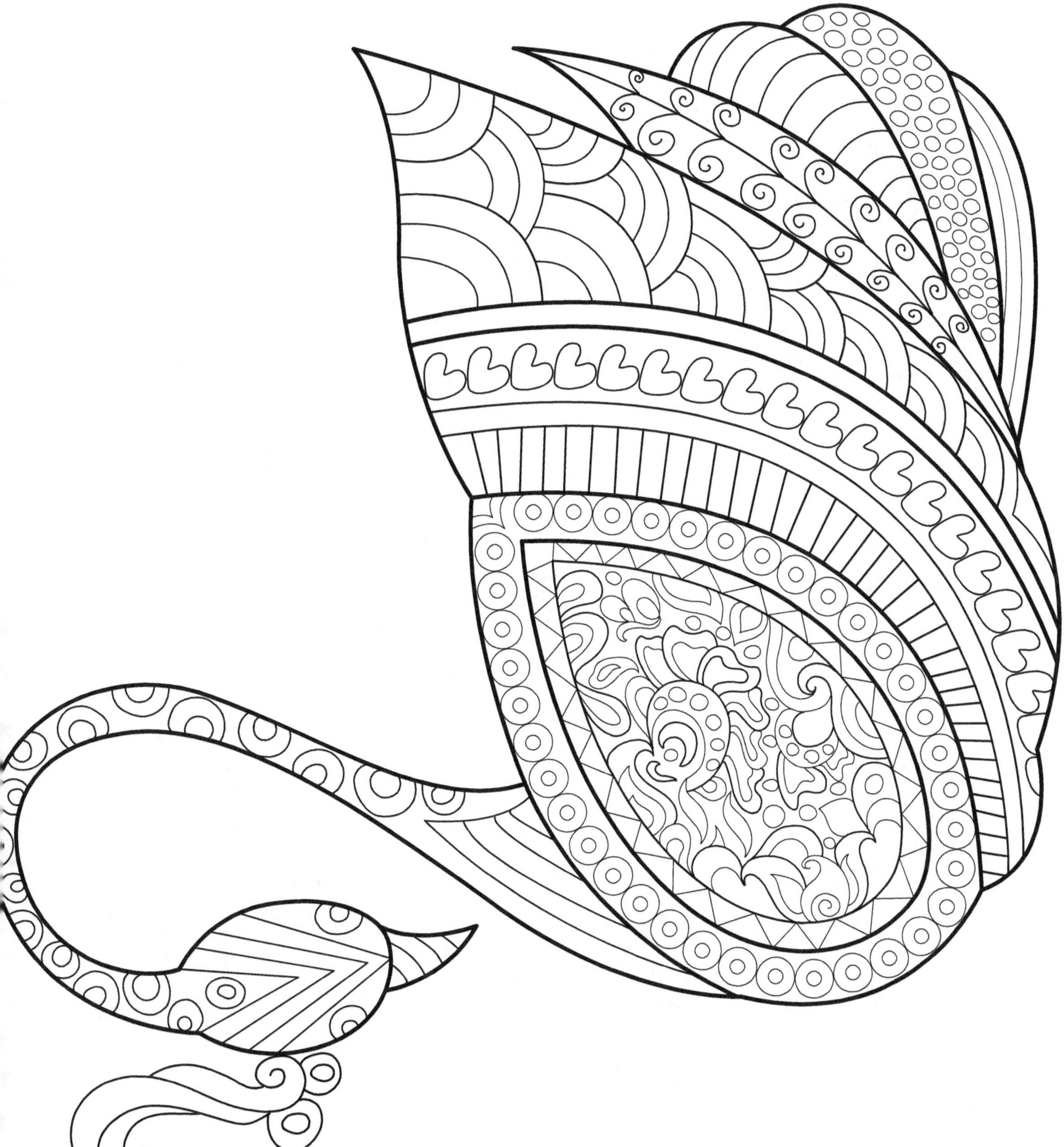

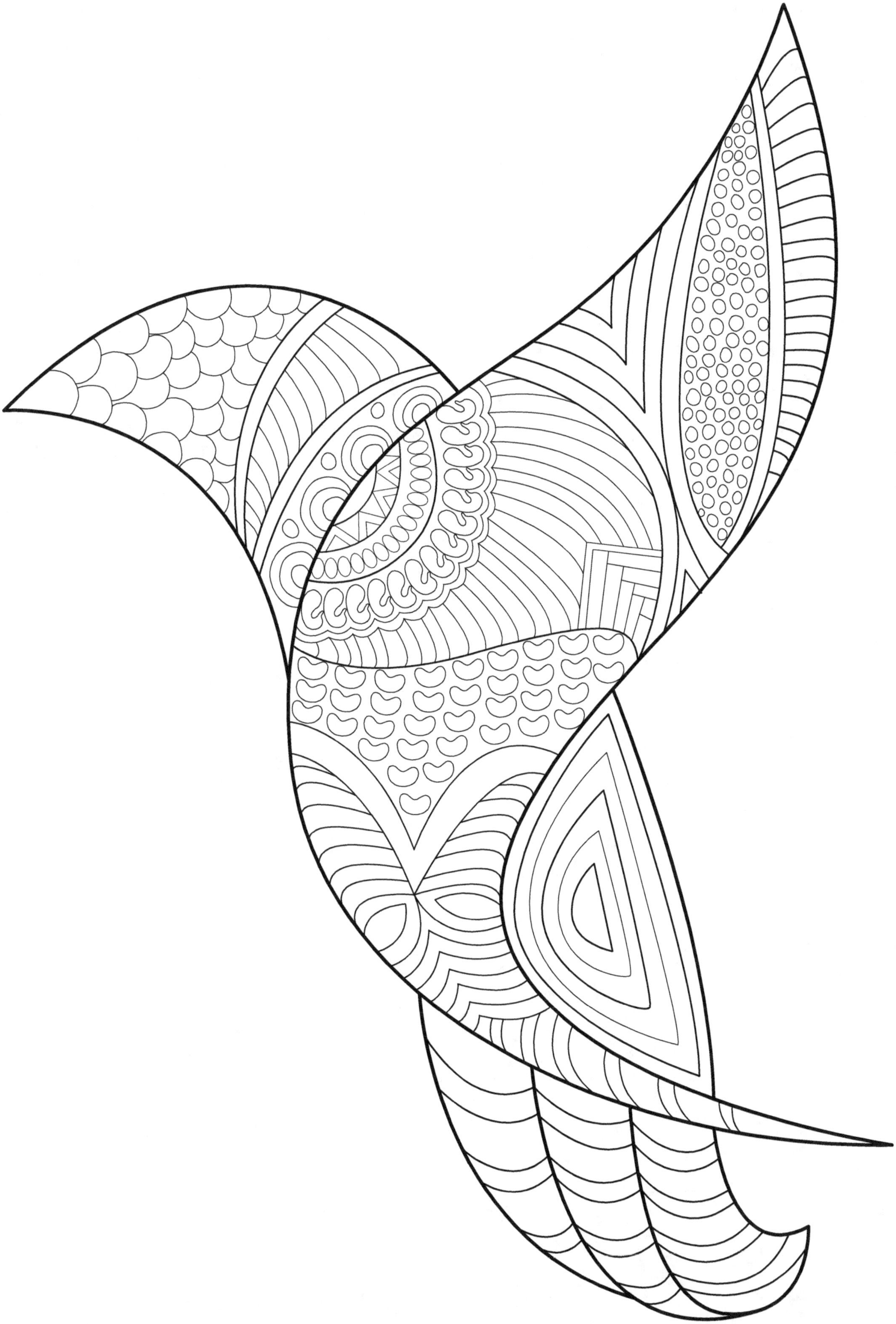

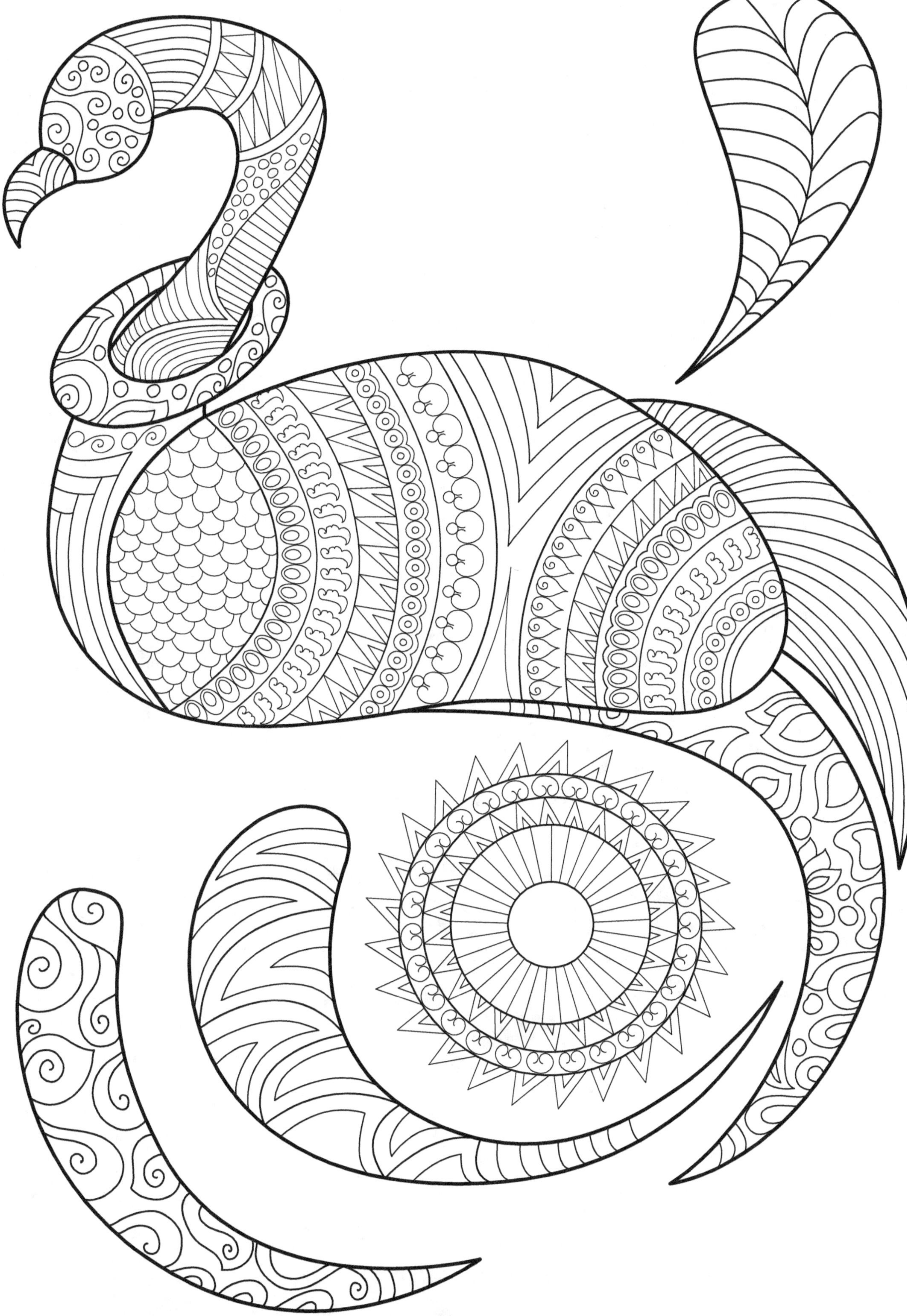

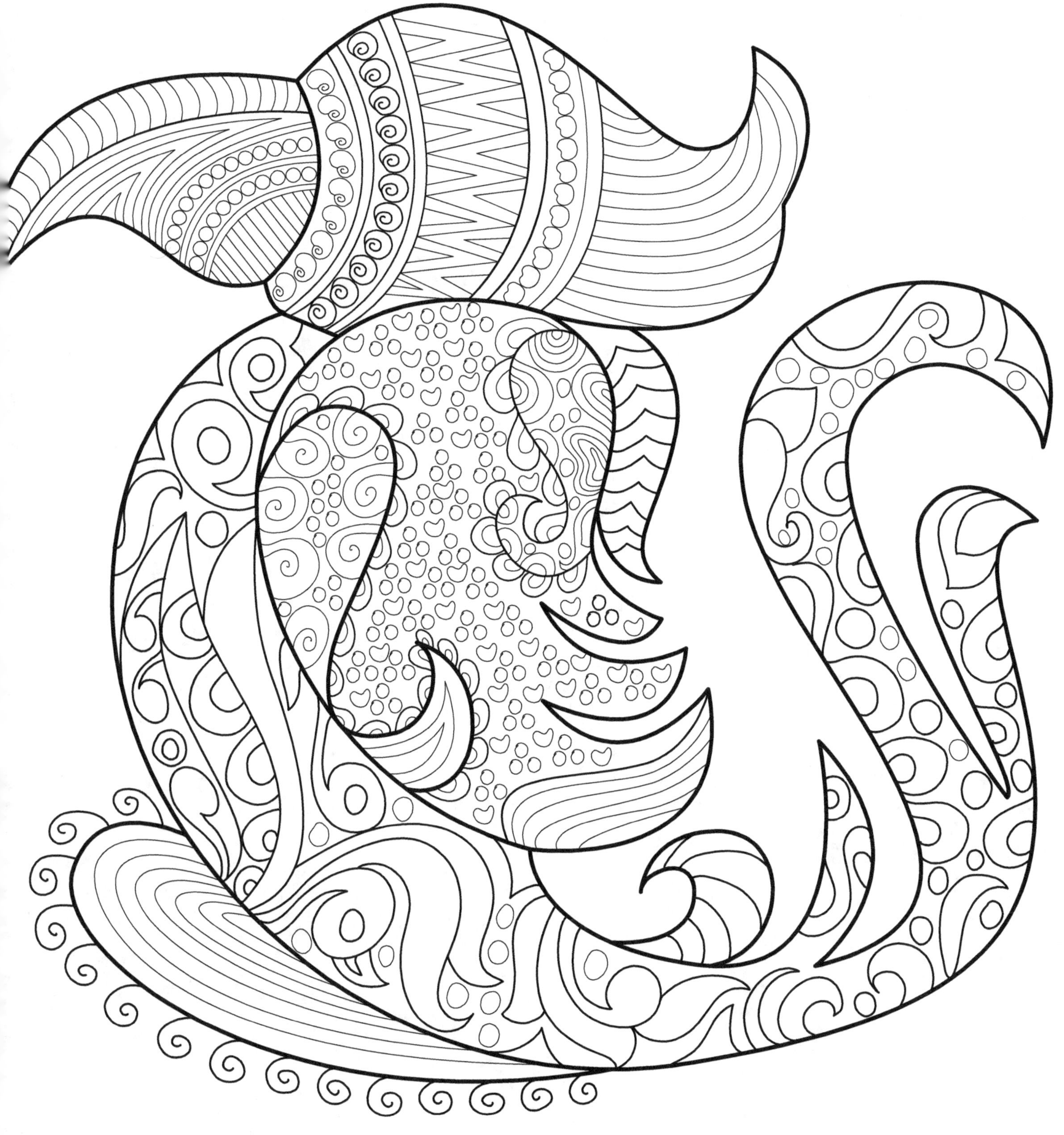

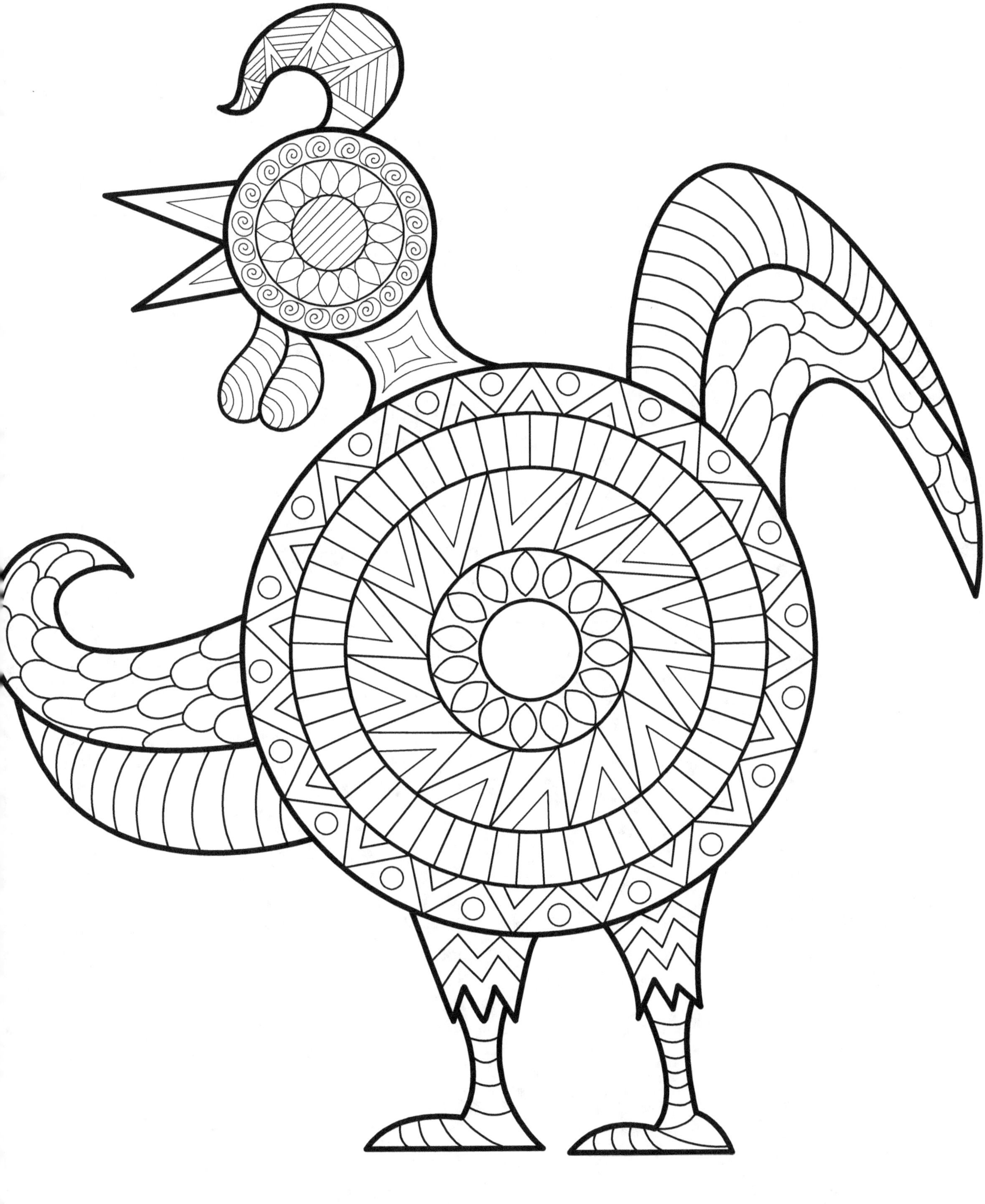

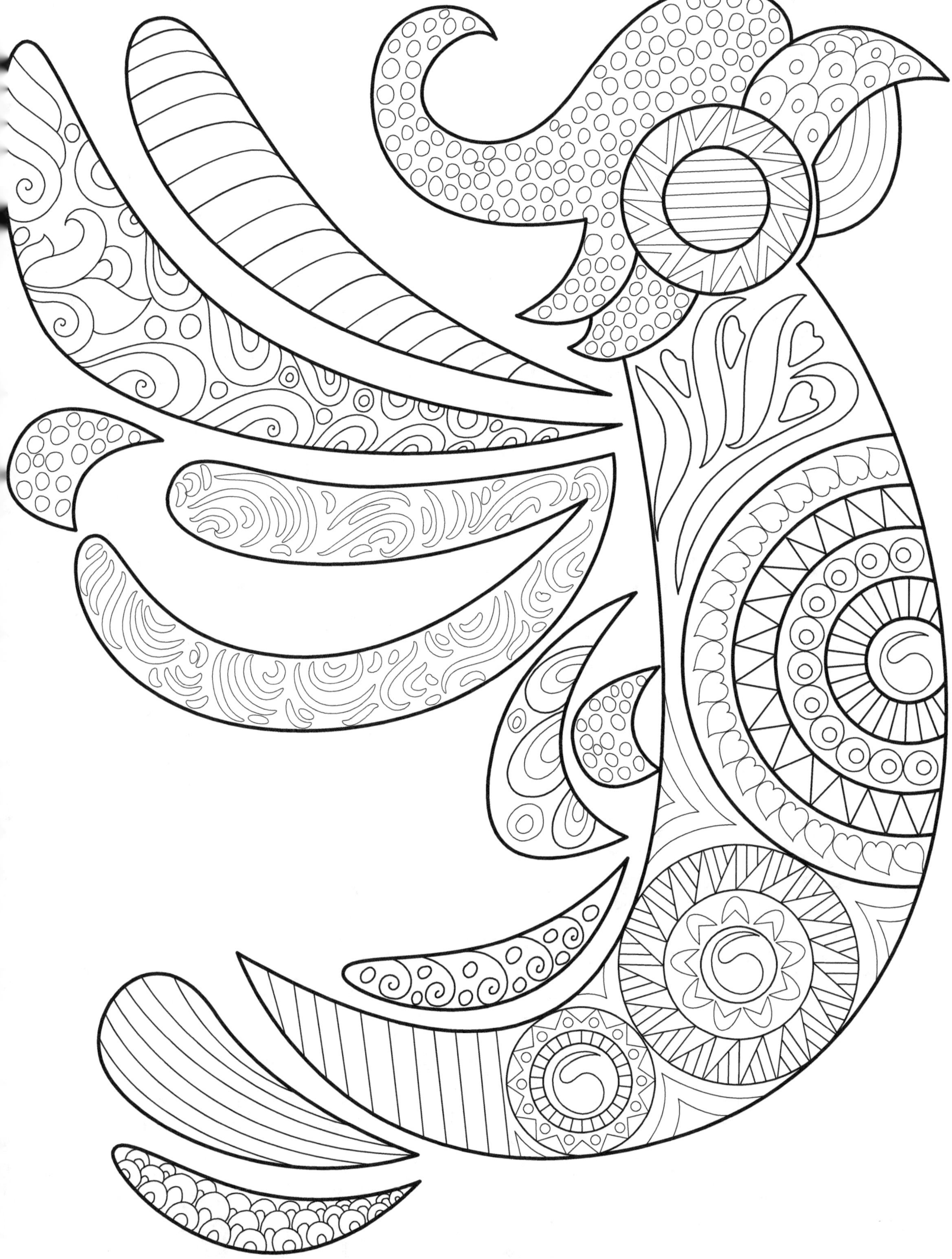

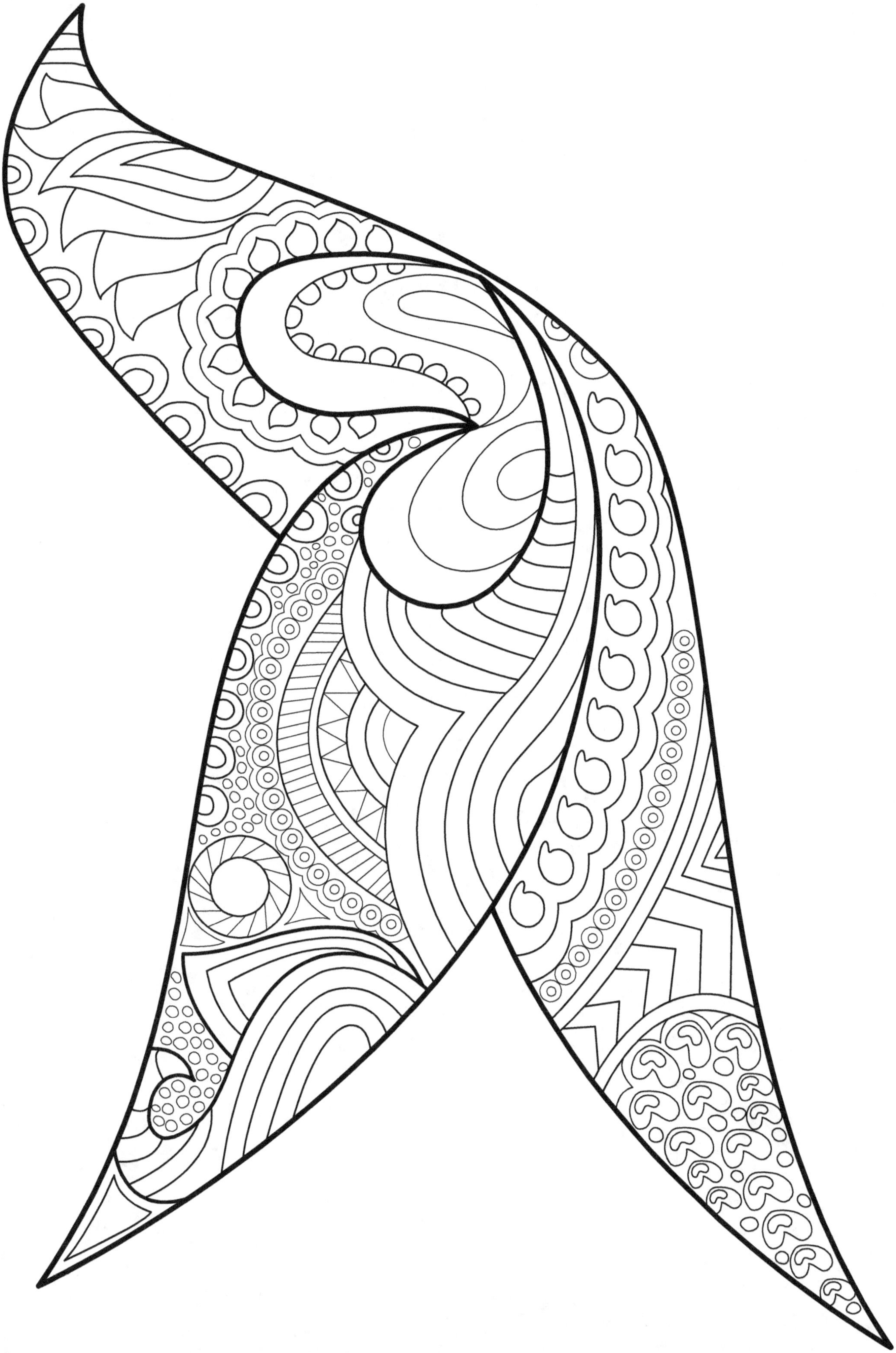

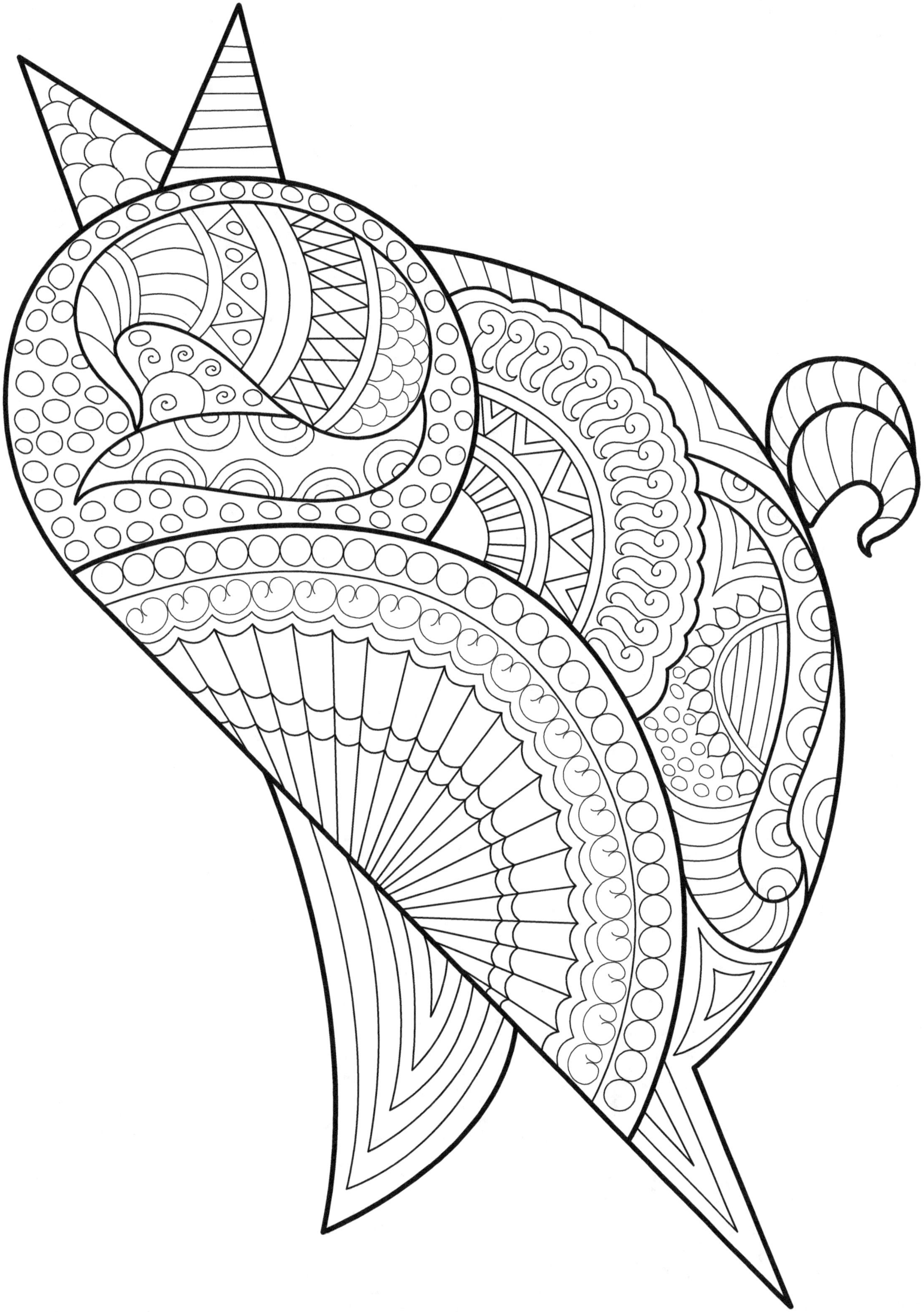

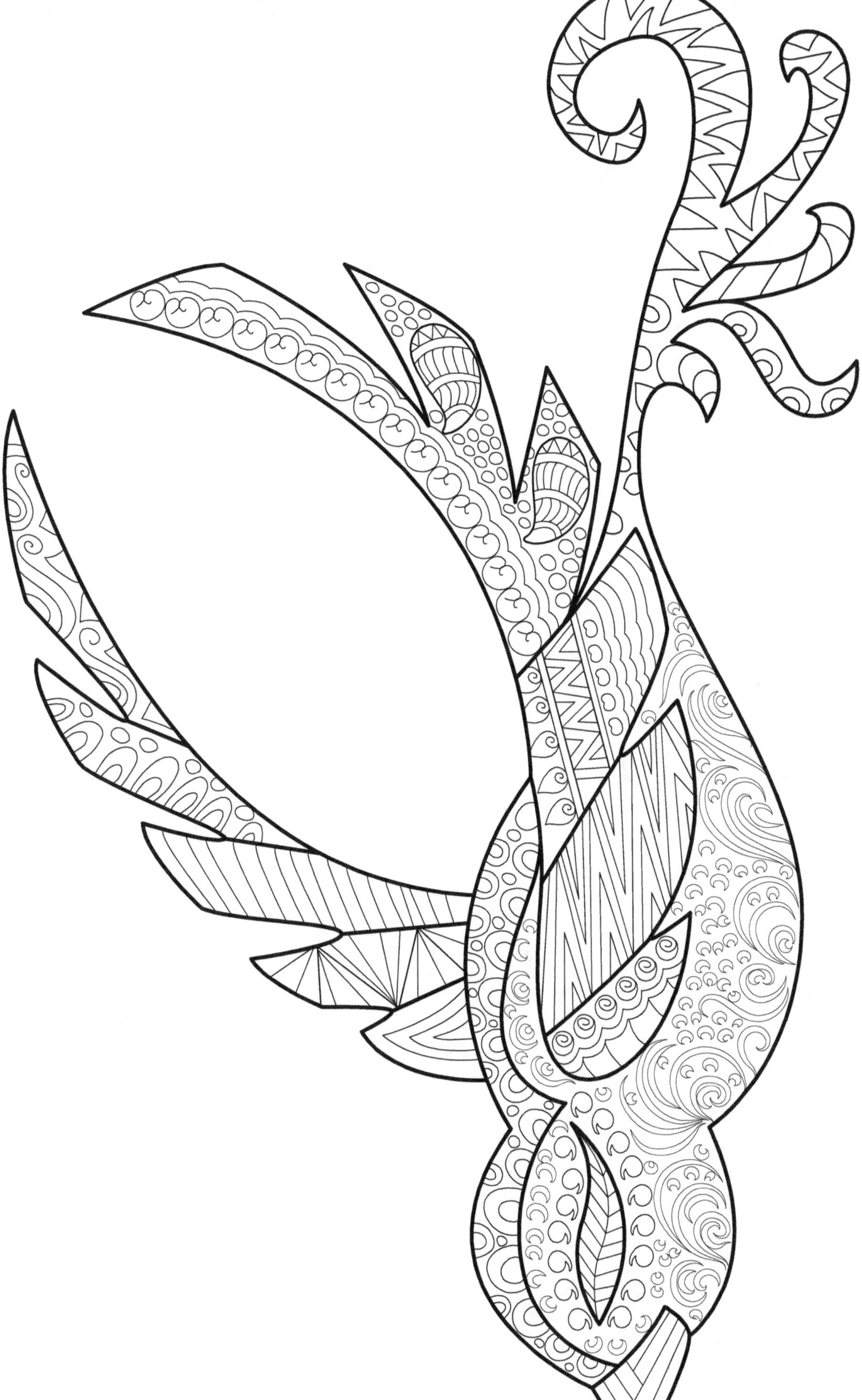

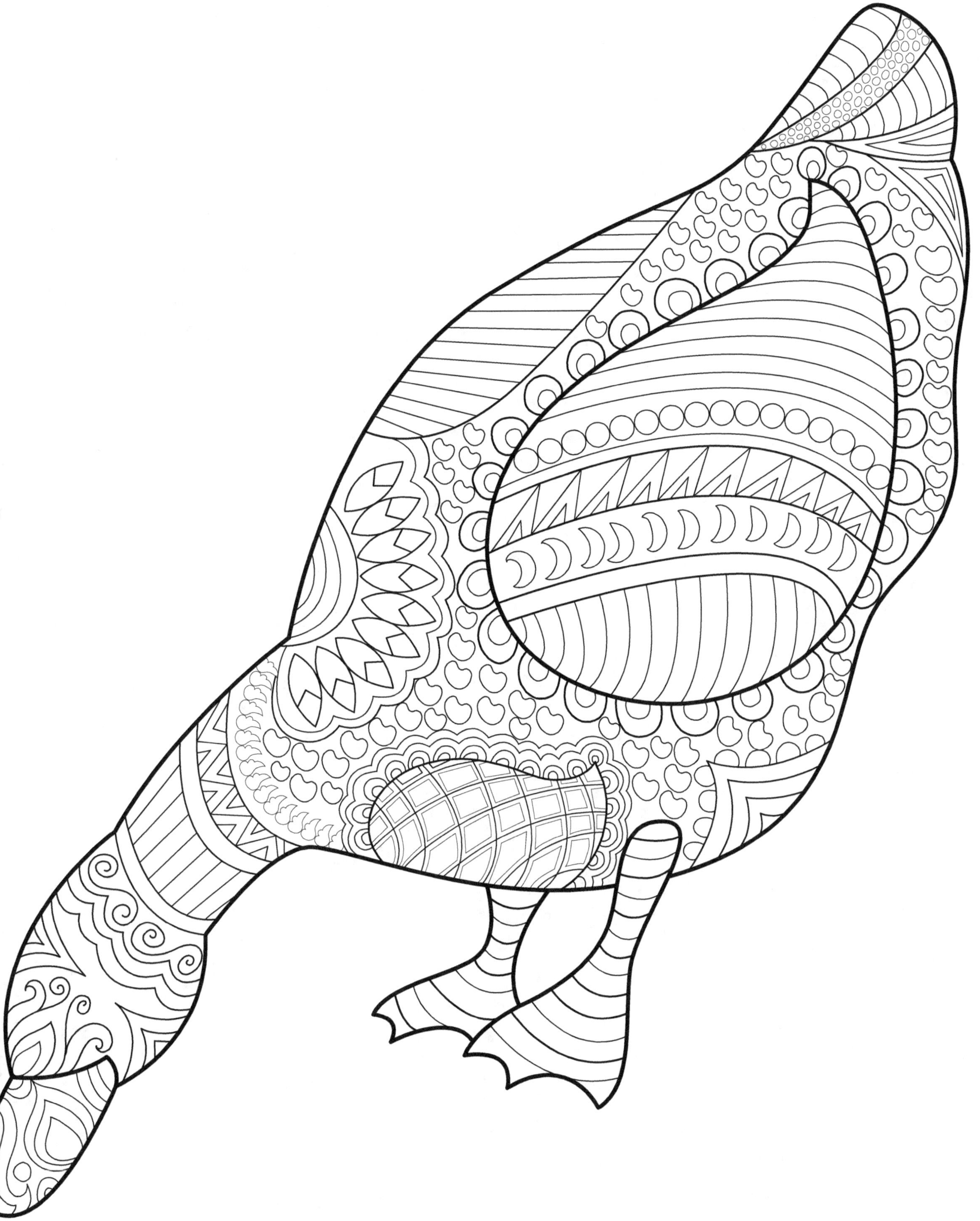

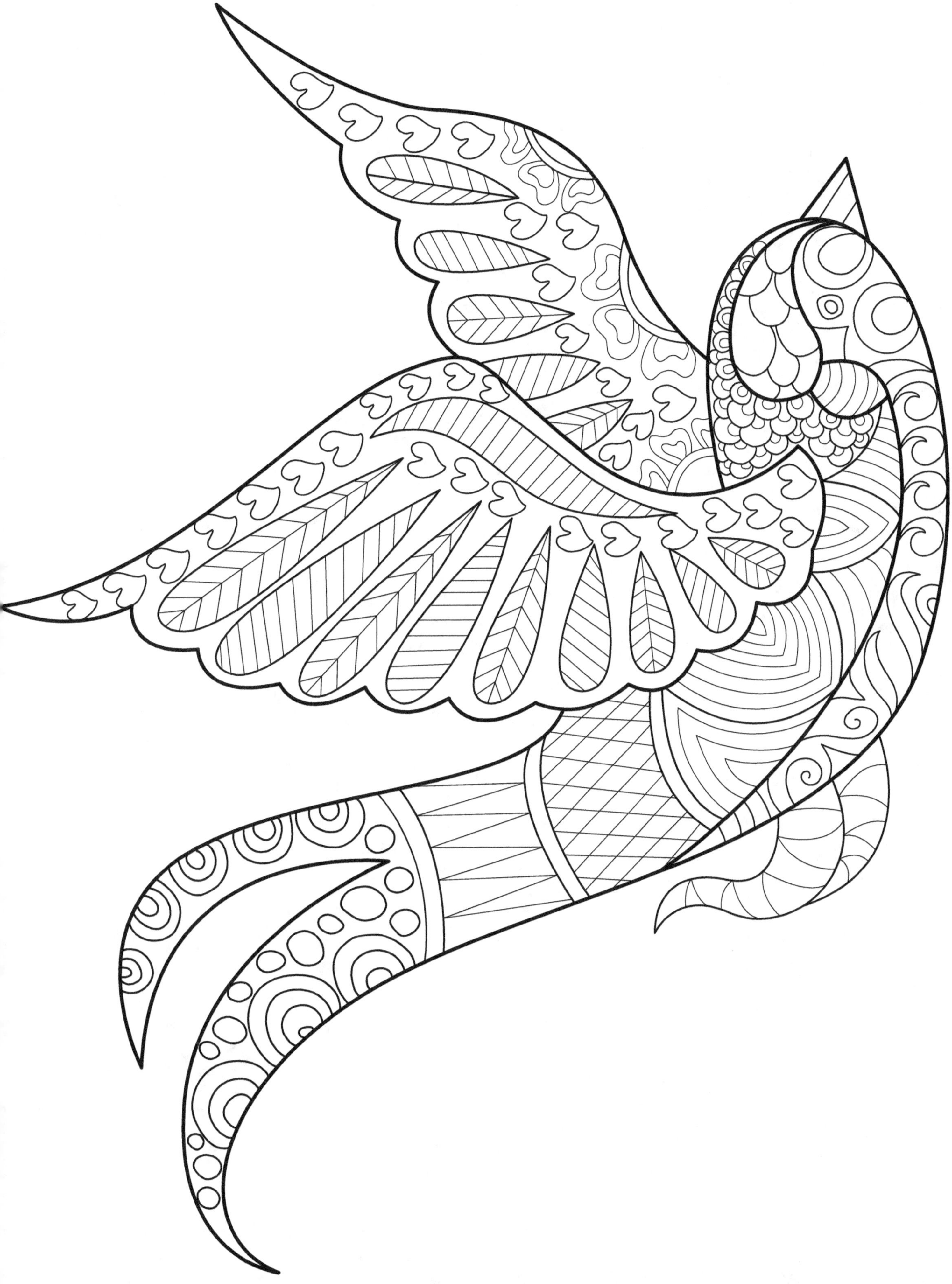

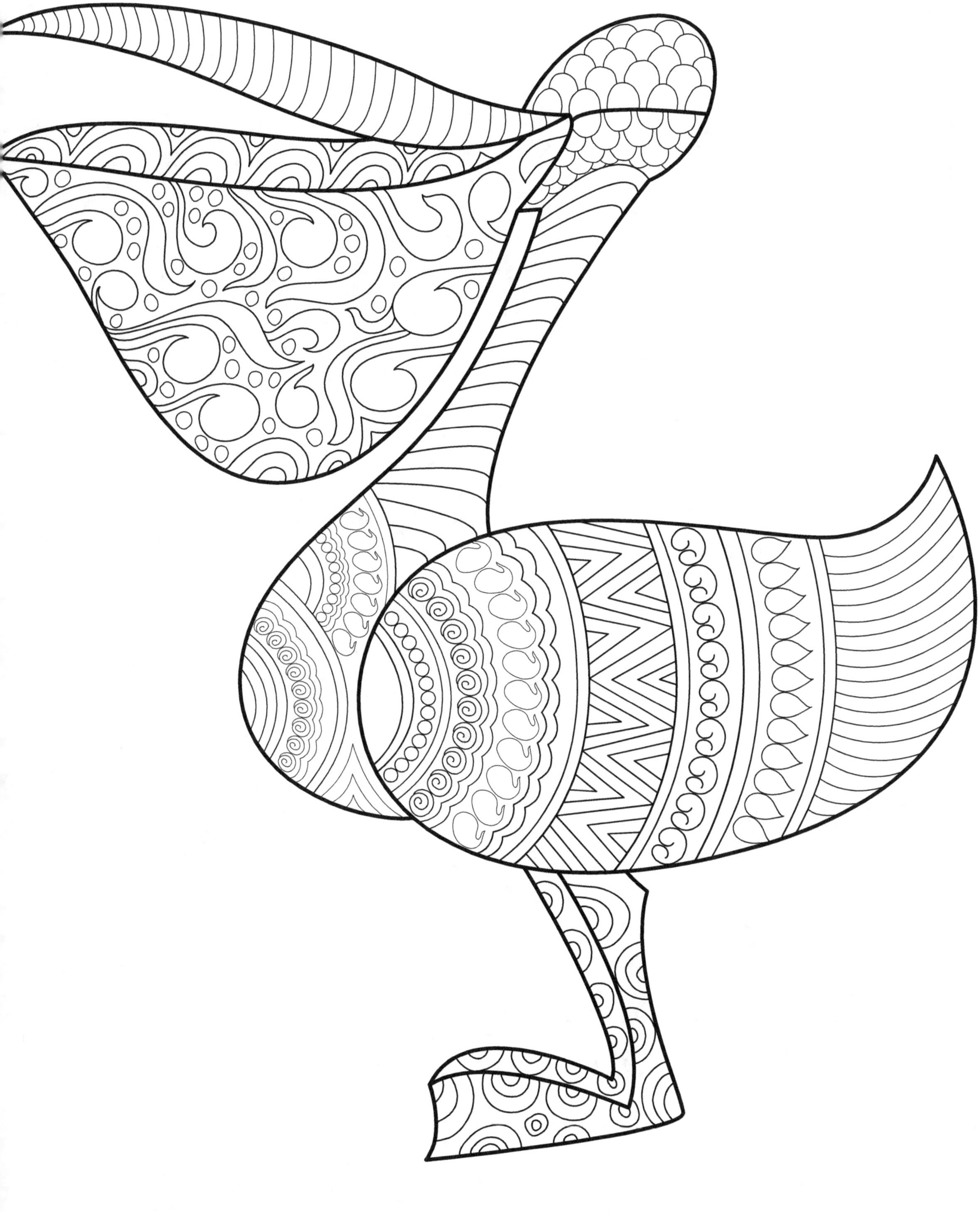

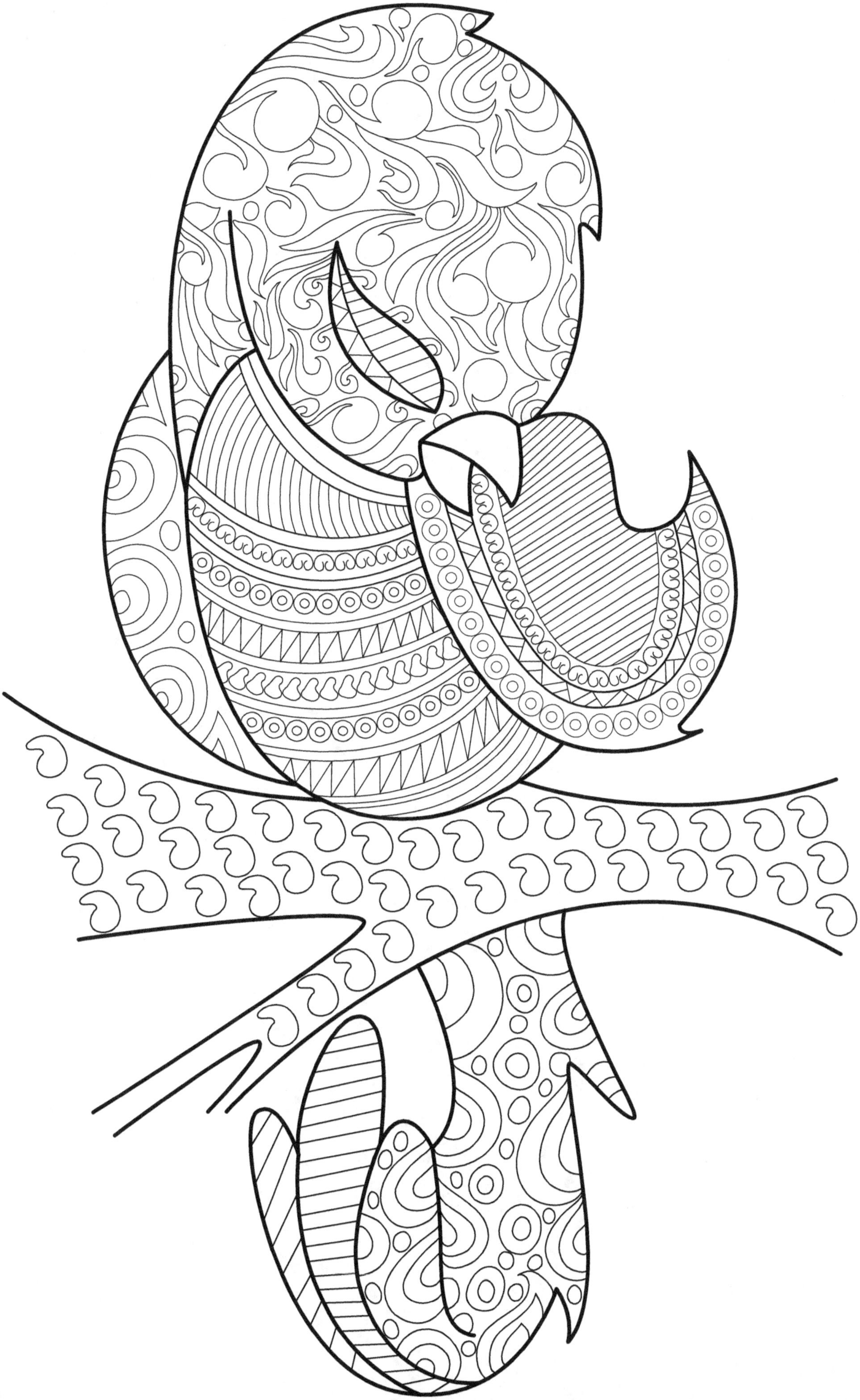

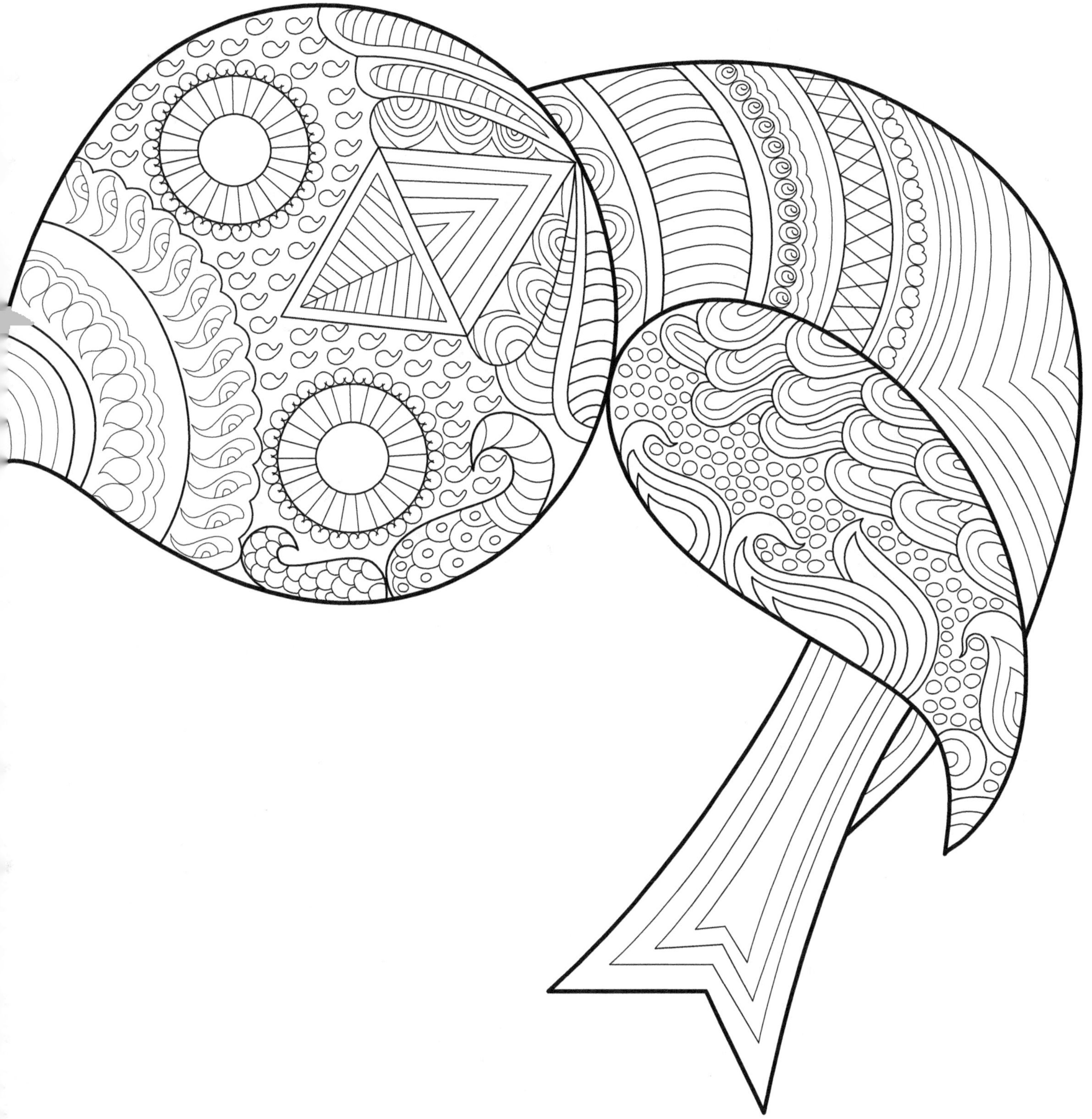

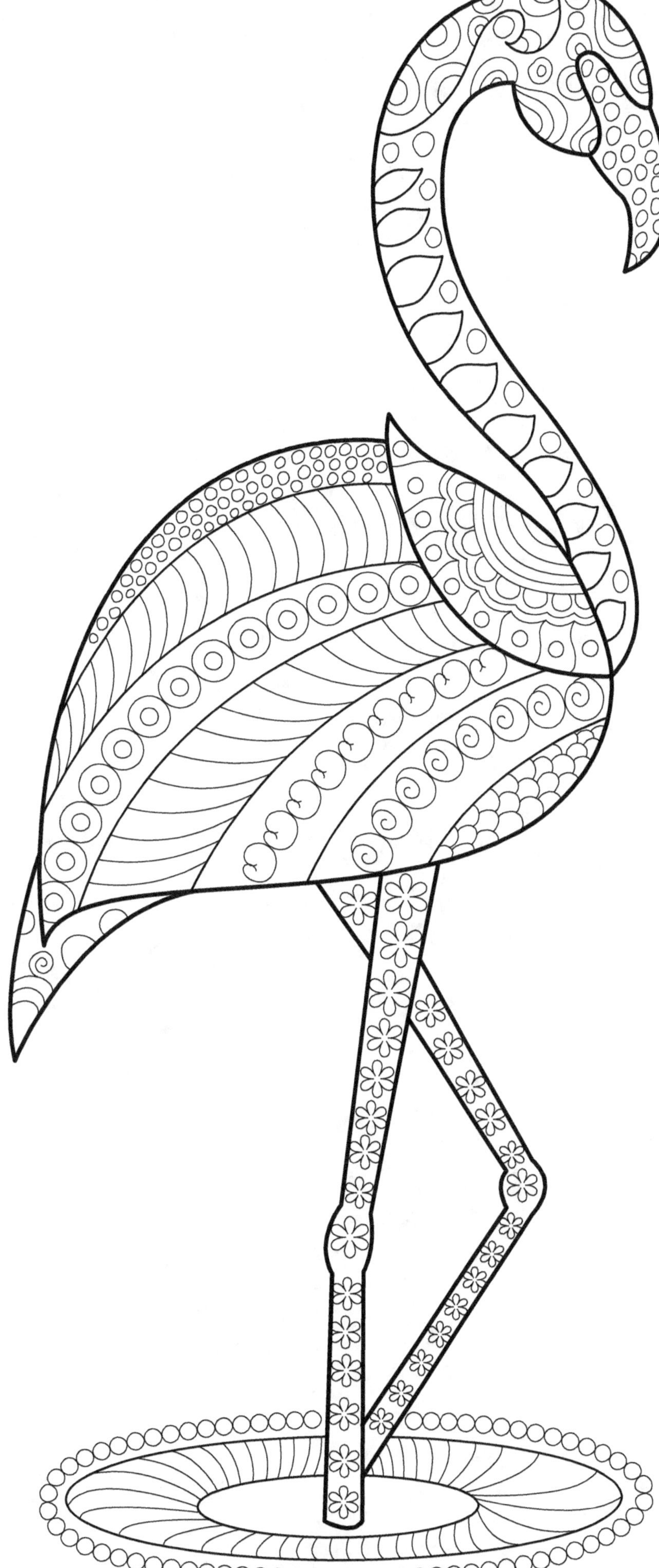

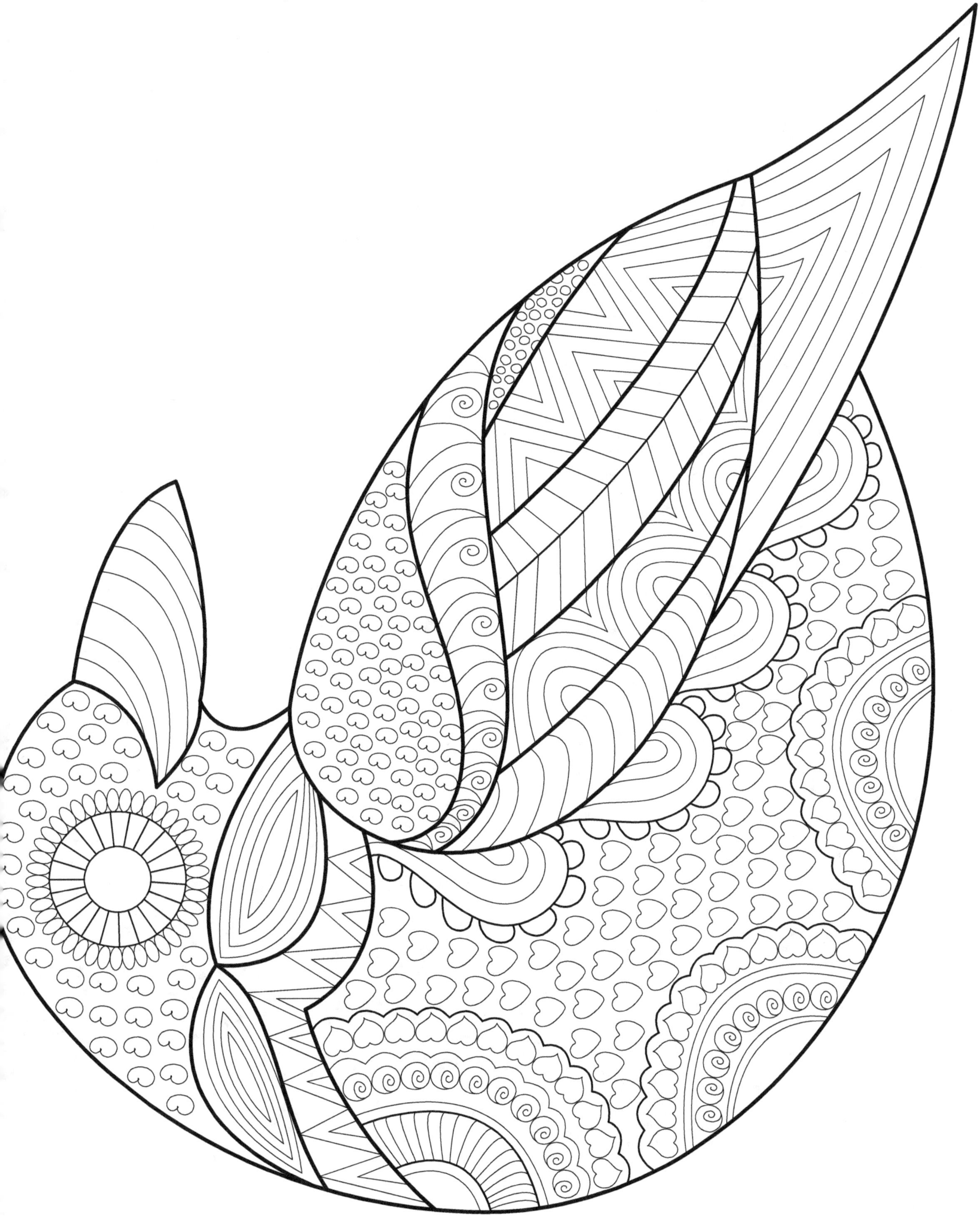

# MAZE

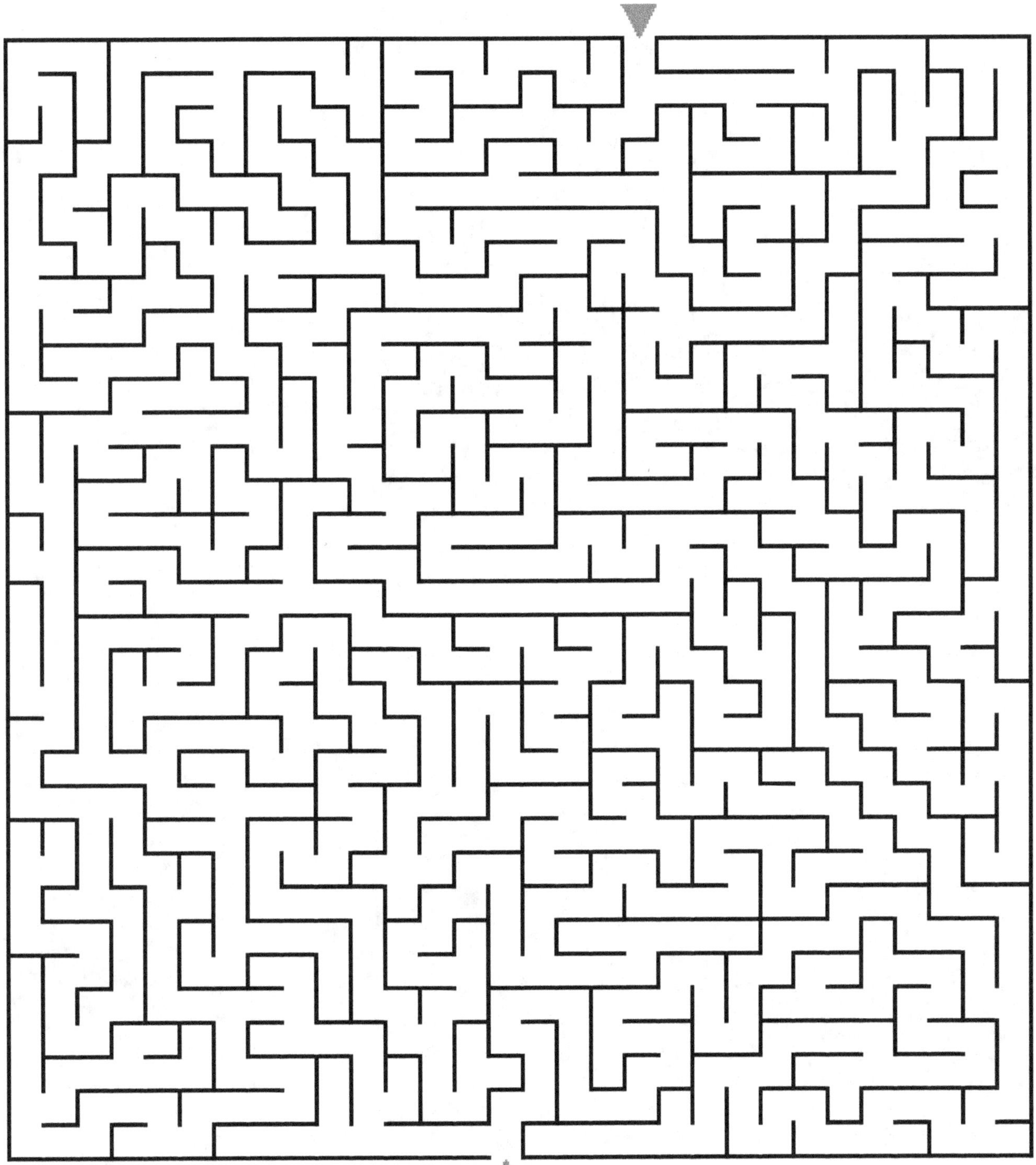

# COLOR CHARTS

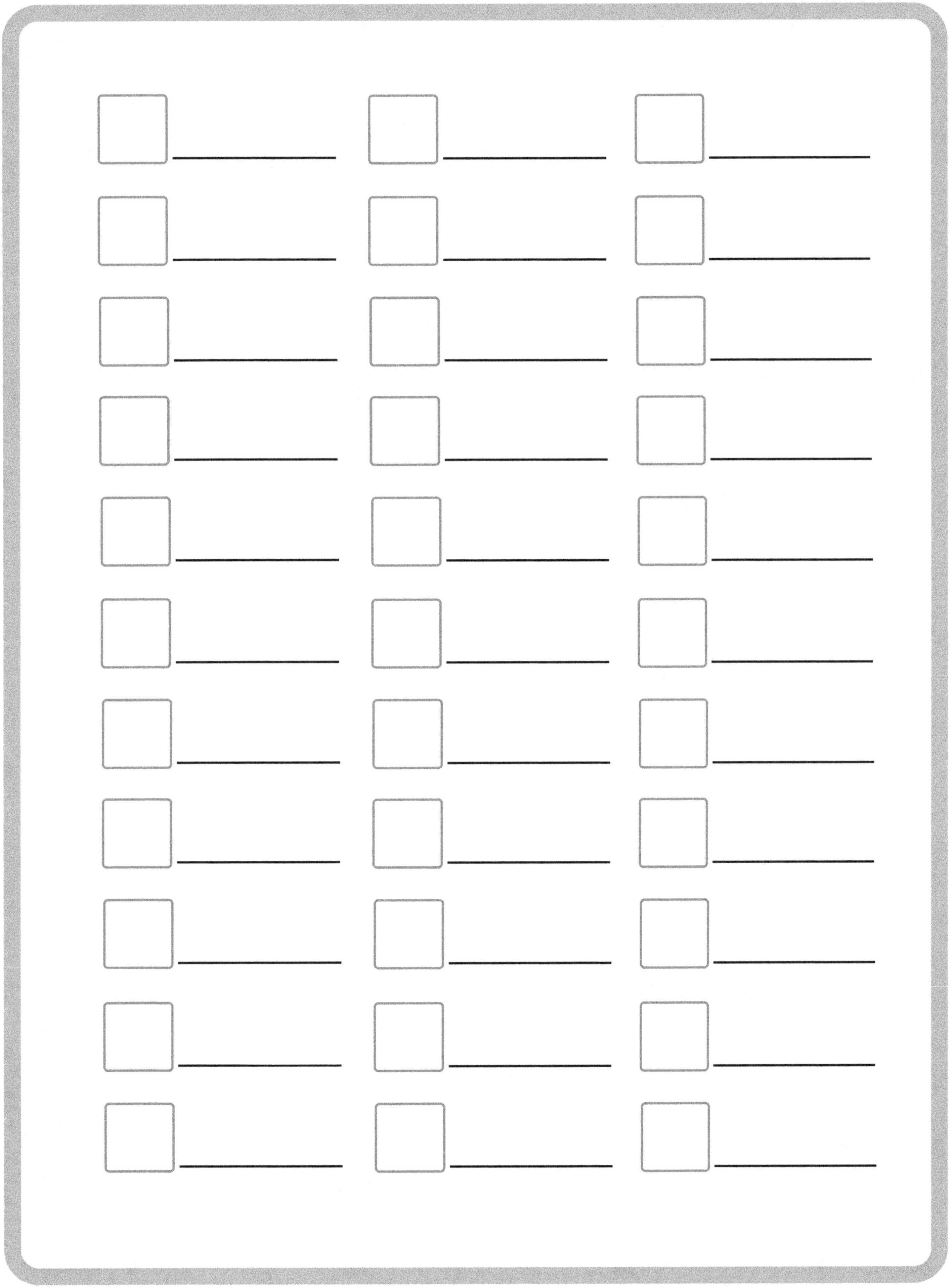

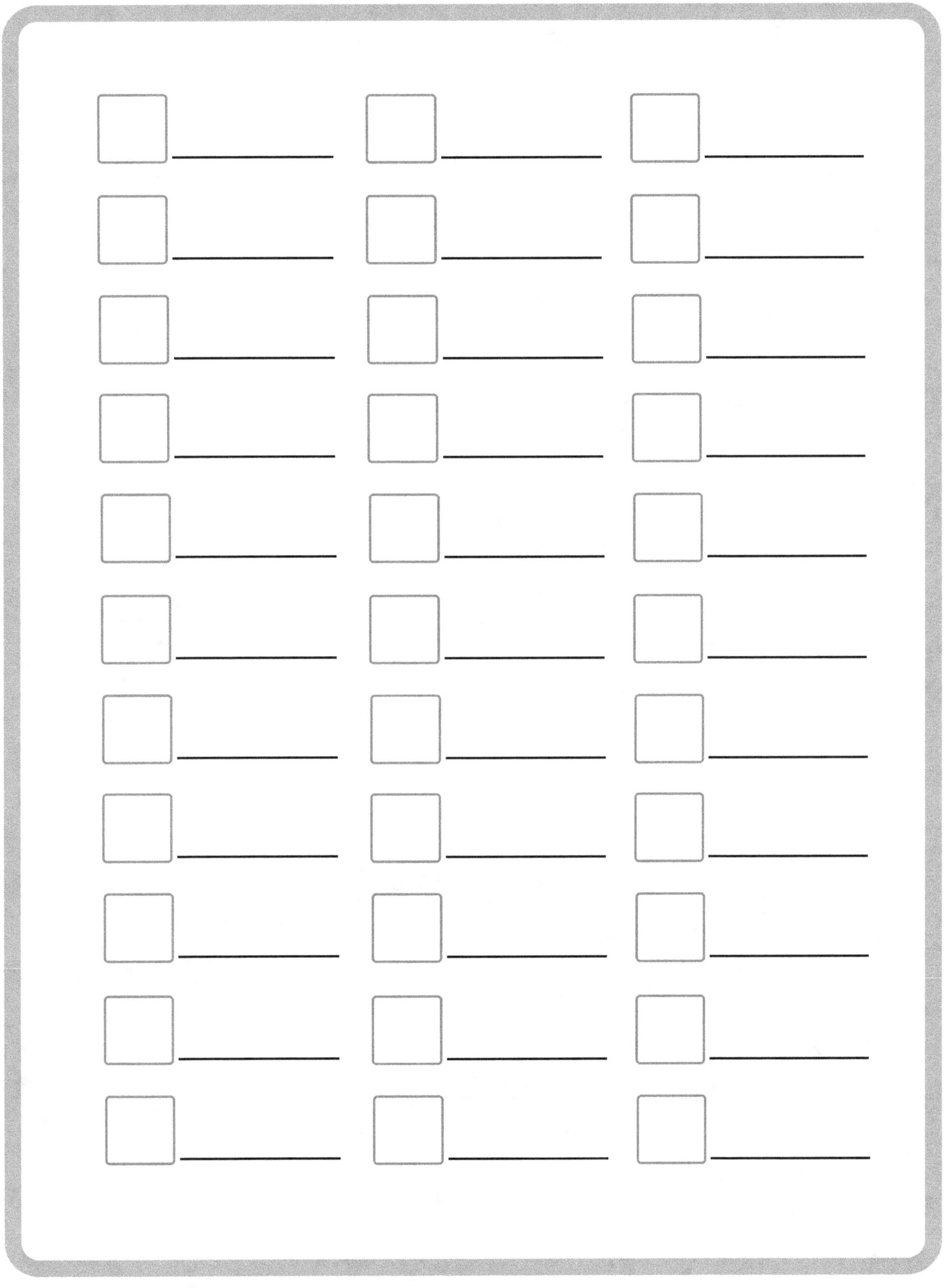

# Solution

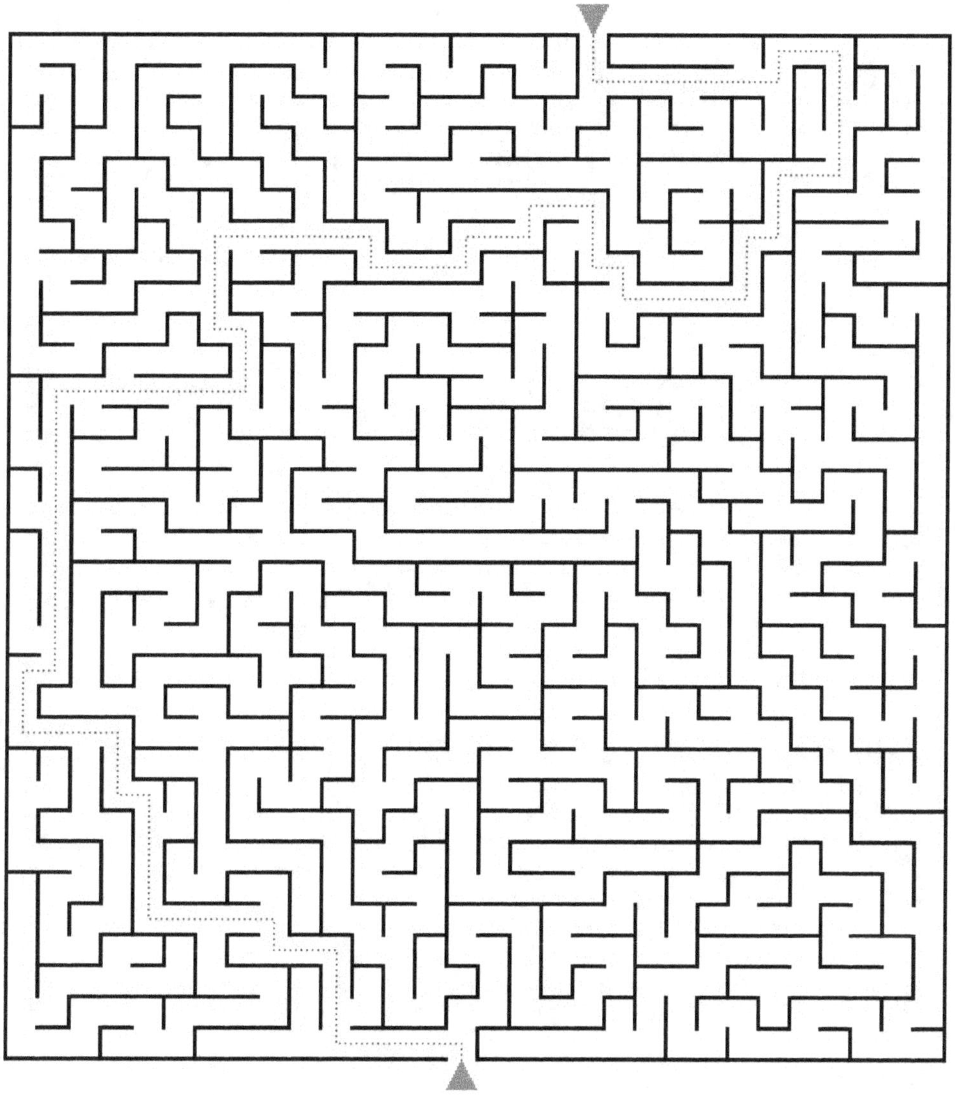

www.ingramcontent.com/pod-product-compliance
Lightning Source LLC
Chambersburg PA
CBHW081452220526
45466CB00008B/2611